Desert
Dancing

*Exploring the Land, the People,
the Legends of the California Deserts*

Happy Trails!

Desert Dancing

*Exploring the Land, the People,
the Legends of the California Deserts*

Len Wilcox

HUNTER

HUNTER PUBLISHING, INC.
130 Campus Drive, Edison, NJ 08818
☎ 732-225-1900; 800-255-0343; fax 732-417-1744
hunterp@bellsouth.net

Ulysses Travel Publications
4176 Saint-Denis, Montréal, Québec
Canada H2W 2M5
☎ 514-843-9882 ext 2232; fax 514-843-9448

Windsor Books
The Boundary, Wheatley Road, Garsington
Oxford, OX44 9EJ England
☎ 01865-361122; fax 01865-361133

ISBN 1-55650-876-X
© 2000 Len Wilcox

Cover image: Death Valley © Index Stock Photography
Maps by Kim André © 2000 Hunter Publishing, Inc.

1   2   3   4

Dedication

For Larry Baca and Suz Counsilman, coworkers and good friends. And for Dally.

Thanks to Steve Grimm and Dennis Casebier for their help with historical research. However, any errors in fact remain my own.

Contents

INTRODUCTION   1
  Exploring the Desert   1
  Desert Allure   6
  About This Book   8
  Eco-Awareness   10

THE MOJAVE   13
  Introduction   13
    The Essence of the Mojave   14
  Last Chance Canyon   18
    Exploring Last Chance Canyon from the South   23
    Exploring Last Chance Canyon from the North   24
  Golden Valley   25
    The Rainbow Chaser   27
  Boron to Randsburg   31
    History   31
    Randsburg Today   32
    Cross-Country to Randsburg   34
    Kangaroo Rats & Other Wildlife   37
  Ridgecrest & Points North   39
    Wild Horses   39
    Cerro Gordo   40
    Bodie   43
  The Land of Dreams   48
  Barstow & the Central Mojave   53
    Rainbow Basin   53
    Barstow   56
  The Mojave National Preserve   61
    Dennis Casebier   66
    Health Resort or Money Machine?   70
    The Singing Sands of the Kelso Dunes   71
  The Mojave Road   72
    Fort Mojave   75
    Travels Along the Mojave Road   76
    Marl Springs   83

DEATH VALLEY   89
  Introduction   89

From the Panamints to the Amargosa 90
 The First Travelers 92
 A Visit to the Racetrack 94
Death Valley Lodging 99
 Hotels & Motels 99
 Camping 100
From Beatty to Ballarat 103
 On the Trail of Shorty Harris 104
 A Visit to Rhyolite & Bullfrog 107
 Ballarat 110
 Shorty's Second Strike 115
The Panamints 118
 The First Strike 119
 Panamint City 121
 Outsmarting the Outlaws 122
Death Valley Scotty 126
Joshua Tree National Park 131
 The Story of Bill Keys 132

THE COLORADO DESERT 139
 Introduction 139
 Juan Bautista de Anza's Passage Across the Desert 140
 Anza-Borrego & Pegleg Smith 142
 The Legend of Pegleg Smith 144
 The Salton Sea 147
 The Salton Sink 147
 The Accident that Created the Salton Sea 148
 Too Much Salt, Too Little Oxygen 149
 The Demand for Water 153
 North of Yuma 154
 Exploring the Picacho Peak Region 156
 The Center of the World 159
 The Blythe Intaglios 161
 We Visit the Mine 164

APPENDIX I 169
 Websites & Addresses 169
 Websites 169
 Mojave Federal Land Management & Park Offices 170
 National Parks 171
 Bureau of Land Management Desert Area Field Offices 171
 BLM Open Areas (Off-Highway Vehicle Areas) 172

APPENDIX II   173
    Desert Travel   173
      Land Use   173
      Desert Driving Tips   174
      Gear & Clothing   175
      Bees & Snakes   176
      Emergency Supplies   176
      Desert Survival   178
      Camping on the Desert   179

APPENDIX III   183
    Mojave Desert State Parks   183
      Red Rock Canyon State Park   184
      Antelope Valley California Poppy Reserve   185
      The Ripley Desert Woodland   185
      Antelope Valley Indian Museum   186
      Saddleback Butte State Park   187
      Mitchell Caverns & the Providence Mountains   187

Maps

Deserts of California   9
Last Chance Canyon   19
Golden Valley   27
Boron to Randsburg   35
Ridgecrest to Points North   42
Barstow & the Central Mojave   55
Death Valley   88
From Beatty to Ballarat   103
Anza-Borrego   143
North of Yuma   155
The Blythe Intaglios   163

Introduction

She calls it desert dancing, what we do out there. It's a place some of us call home, no matter where we live; a place you go back to, even when you've never been there before. Deserts around the world may be different, but the feeling is the same; the hearts of prophets and devils alike beat stronger there. A place you feel eternity. Home for the spirit.

Forbidding – to some. Bleak and lonely. No desert rat can deny these feelings at times.

That's part of it. It's also the primordial challenge of surviving, low-tech life and death, surrounded by a rugged, powerful beauty and the wonderful adaptations of Mother Nature to the difficult, dry world of the desert. Animals that can live their whole lives without a drink of water. Seeds that can lay dormant for years, then germinate after a desert rainstorm that offers just enough water to bring them to life.

The more high-tech my tools and toys, the more I need my desert time, my desert dancing.

Exploring the Desert

Some trips we hardly get off the pavement. Like this last time. We crossed out of the Central Valley over the Tehachapis, leaving behind the fog and agribusiness bustle about the time we passed by the Arvin exit. The **Tehachapi Loop** is beyond.

The loop is a place where the railroad makes a big circle around a hill, crosses over itself, climbing to gain altitude to get over the summit. It doesn't sound interesting, but watching 80-car trains, six or eight engines roaring and rumbling, inching their way up and around the loop, the engines and first cars passing over the tail, is a sight. It's man conquering the mountain, ingeniously devising a way to go with machines that shouldn't be able to get there – and real power at work.

Stop here sometime. Get yourself a sub sandwich in Bakersfield – or if you're coming the other way, Mojave – and a six-pack of your favorite beverage. Then prepare to sit and rest awhile. Take the exit at Keene; follow the two-lane around to the overlook on the side of the hill. Park over by the sign, sit down and be patient (which is why you brought the six-pack). It sometimes takes a while, but while you're waiting, other tourists, mostly train hobbyists, will come by. Talk to them, and you may learn the history of the Tehachapi Loop. Soon, from far-off, you'll hear a rumble and a whine. Then a train gradually materializes, climbing the hill from the west. It'll slowly make the loop and, if it's a big one, cross over itself roaring like a dragon eating its tail.

I don't know why it's a thrill, but it is.

The train rumbles on to **Mojave**, and so do we, but on a four-lane highway. At the cement mine east of Tehachapi the countryside changes, from Sierra pines and oaks to desert scrub. Tall, stately Joshuas appear and, in spring, carry proudly their beautiful white, waxy blossoms.

The Joshua grows very slowly. A few inches a year, decades to grow a few feet; a tough old tree, older than you and me put together, may only be 10 feet tall. Don't expect much shade from these old guys; they are desert-thin and wiry, prickly with long, slender shards for leaves. Don't fight with them, either. They'll win.

And there's creosote. The quintessential desert dweller, creosotes aren't worth anything to men, but to the desert they are home and shelter to many creatures. They are smart, too, spacing themselves out with a root system that sinks dozens of feet and spreads to grab every drop of water that might come their way. These roots provide an infrastructure for the soil, and animals will burrow under the creosote bush to make underground homes. Jackrabbits live in the bushes, taking comfort in the shade and nibbling on the branches. They don't eat the small, waxy leaves; those are pungent and bitter.

Dropping down onto the desert, on the left is **Barren Ridge**, a place that lives up to its name. It's criss-crossed with jeep trails, all of which I want to take. But not so my desert-dancing partner. She doesn't like cliffs, and we've ventured far enough up the ridge to know the drop-offs are significant.

Gem Hill isn't as bad. We went there, last trip.

It's located west of Rosamond, just north of the Tropico Mine. From Tropico, go north on Mojave-Tropico road, past the mine, and after a mile or so there'll be a neat-looking hill with trails. We first took a little-used bladed cut – probably a fire line, not really a trail, I later decided – up to the crest of the first small peak north of the mine. We stopped, dug out the binoculars and a couple of sandwiches, and sat on the sand to take in the sights.

South and east, the highly developed Antelope Valley spreads like a chancre on the face of the desert. Trails have turned into paved streets, houses and businesses have replaced creosote and cactus, minivans putter along where jackrabbits no longer forage. There's no sense of peace in that direction. But to the northwest another hill beckons, with a small valley leading into a saddle between peaks. This valley kept claiming our attention, calling out to be explored.

After lunch, we returned to the Tropico road and found the access trail to our beckoning hills to the northwest. Numerous small trails crossed our road, and of course the scenery is much different at ground level than it was from the peak. But we found the path to the valley and the saddle.

Spring flowers lit the dry watercourses and guided us around the hills through a place that was almost a small canyon, with desert cliffs on the north and south sides of us. The cliffs to the south were especially interesting: numerous small caves in the conglomerate rock, and the white stains below the caves told us they were the perches of large, predatory birds, either eagles or hawks. Markings on the cliff could be ancient petroglyphs; they were high up, however, so they would be very ancient.

With the binoculars we studied the cliff face. The petroglyphs were made up of colored rock stuck in the conglomerate cliff. At the bottom of the cliff face was a digging, under a rock overhanging, that looked interesting. Was it a mine? A trail climbed to the cliff face, then wandered left past a window rock and up to the peak.

It was steep, very steep, and my desert dancer Suz shuddered, then said we could go up there if I wanted, and see close-up what this place was about. I reluctantly said no, the trail was a bit much.

We climbed in and Mr. Jeep – Suz's pet name for the truck – disagreed with me. It took the trail, and we climbed to the cliff face.

Someday I ought to get an incline meter, to find out if we really did go straight up on this trail. I'm known for coloring up my facts a little when I talk about my trail rides; Suz thinks my stories aren't always the way things are, but the way they ought to be. I think she's wrong, but I'll admit that my reality is different from hers. In the interest of editorial integrity, let's just say it was steep. That's colorless, but factual.

At the bottom of the cliff face, the story the ground told was different from anywhere we'd been on the desert. There was grass, lots of deep-green grass, freshly watered from the El Niño spring we were experiencing. The rock overhang wasn't just a digging, it was a campsite. Its roof was smoke-tainted from many campfires.

A foot trail went up around the left side of the cliff, and had been used by daring trail bike riders. On the right side were numerous rocks and bushes, an inviting desert panoply of rocks awaiting investigation. We chose the right side to explore.

Just above the rocks, in the gravelly moraine at the bottom of the cliff, hundreds or perhaps thousands of tiny bones told of successful hunts by the hawks who lived above us. We knew they were hawks, not eagles, because of the three feathers we found on the ground, in the grassy area where the soil has been enriched by hundreds of years' worth of bird droppings.

We slowly and carefully climbed around the cliff face, finding some interesting bits of mica, fool's gold, and a bit of opal or opalite – I'm not certain which. As we hunted, a curious discomfort edged into the back of my mind. We were invading the hawks' territory, entering their home, and while we were there, they would have to be elsewhere. The peace and privilege of sharing their habitat was powerful, but we did not want to stay long and wear out our welcome.

Someday we'll return to this magic little valley, and set ourselves across from the hawk's home and wait for them to return. We'll camp where we can study him and her with binoculars, far enough away that we won't be too much of an intrusion.

This is our desert dancing. It's the sum of all we do out there, out in what some call the badlands; whether it's rockhounding, watching hawks, exploring a trail, hunting for gold, or watching the clouds. It's the experience of being in this strange and harsh land. Whenever our daily lives become a little too much, we know it is time to go.

Today, our journey ended with a golden sunset as we slowly made our way down the hill and back to spend the night in the bustle of Antelope Valley. We would come back someday, for another round of desert dancing.

Teakettle Junction.

Desert Allure

Beautiful, wild and free, the desert is one of the last great wildernesses, a place of startling contrasts and raw beauty. Nature collides with itself here, and the results of these collisions are not hidden under a layer of vegetation. They are there for all to see: the geologic forces of uplifting faults, plate tectonics, the ebb and flow of glaciers and oceans, the magic carving of windblown sand, the steady gravity-driven logic of water. Here we can step back in time. Here we meet nature face to face.

I grew up on the desert. For years I knew its ways. I knew the feel of the dry, dry wind, the angry sting of sand, the gritty feel of dust behind the neck – and the sharp, strong colors, deep blue skies, the orange and purple of a desert sunrise, the intense, raw beauty. It was home. Then I went away for decades. Life brings us back to the places we love, however, and I returned many years later. It was a different desert. But the feelings it evoked were the same.

For me, the desert is a spiritual home. I find peace in the wide-open spaces. The innumerable four-wheeling trails revive my freedom-loving spirit. I make new friends with the flora and fauna of the dry lands, and come to respect and love the natural world more each trip. The old mining towns take me back in time, and the hunts for gold or special rocks or the places that made desert history satisfy my need for adventure.

I know I'm not alone in this; the desert has a mystical allure, an attraction that brings people such as you and me together. Prophets and crazy people love the desert for the spiritual forces they feel there. Normal people like us may not go as far as they do, but we know there is a magnetic attraction in the colorful sands, open vistas, and rock ledges. You feel the fascination, or you wouldn't be reading this book. It's not something we can discuss easily, or with those who don't feel it. But it is there.

The deserts of the Southwest are incredibly beautiful lands if you take the time to know them. For the people who just rush by on the freeways, hurrying through the badlands to get to the magical cities of California, the snow playgrounds of Colorado and Utah, or the gambling meccas of Nevada, these are just ugly, dry, boring places with nothing to offer.

How wrong they are, but you can't tell them that; desert lovers, wherever they are, are born with the song of the wind in their souls. The desert hides its secrets from those who don't care to learn them. You can drive from Los Angeles to Las Vegas a hundred times and never see a thing, or, as the current counter-culture would put it, you can find your bliss out here. This is home, even if you've never been here before.

Something about the desert attracts oddball characters. Prophets, prospectors, heroes and outlaws all can find a place in the badlands; there's room for all of us. The stereotype desert rat prospects alone, a hermit whose mule today is a Jeep with air conditioning and an automatic transmission. At least, that's my mule. Purists might want me to use a 1940s military-style GP (General Purpose) vehicle, but I like my creature comforts. When I head for the hills, I'm not out to tear up the desert with an expensive toy. I want to go on trails, and a good sport-utility will take a careful driver most of the places he'd want to go, and do it in air-conditioned comfort. It's only if you want to crawl up the steepest rocks and through the toughest canyons that you need a jacked-up, tricked-out, rough-riding four-wheel-drive.

I'm a born desert rat, and I invite you to come along to some of my favorite places. We'll meet Rainbow Chasers, the early prospectors who spent their lives in search of the big strike. And we'll spend some time with other desert characters, including some magnificent con men and stage robbers. We will see the desert laugh at them all, keeping its character and integrity no matter what the people do upon it. We'll meet some of the current generation of Rainbow Chasers and Desert Dancers – the people who live and play on the desert today.

About This Book

This book isn't a travel guide, although I've tried to make it useful with information and advice on where to go and what to do. It is a journal of my personal exploration into the fascinating history and geology of the desert. In a quest to understand the history and the people of our desert, I talked to dozens of people and read countless books, ranging from home-published pamphlets to scholarly tomes, and am amazed at the various ways the legends of the desert have changed. A Rainbow Chaser who is a hero in one book, a bum in another. The stories have changed with each telling, and each book seems to contradict the other. Some of the books tell the story of the West as it should have been, not as it was. I like the legends, but the beauty is in the truth.

I try to avoid the pitfalls of irresistible legends, and strive for historical accuracy even at the expense of a good story. That's difficult, because the trail is getting cold and the legends of the Rainbow Chasers are great fun. I've had a lot of help in seeking out the truth for this book, however, any errors of fact are my own.

We'll start our journeys on the western **Mojave Desert**. This is high desert, a place that is not so terribly hot in summer that a person can't live with it. In winter, there can be snowstorms, or rains that flood out the roads and make travel interesting. But the weather is fine, if a little warm, most of the year, and it's an area rich in history and beautiful geography.

Then we'll head up to the **Panamints** and **Death Valley**. Geographically, Death Valley should be considered part of the Mojave Desert, but it is a unique place that rates its own section. Death Valley is no place to be in summer, with temperatures reaching 120° or more; it deserves its name. Yet foreign tourists seem to love Death Valley in summer. You'll seldom hear American English or Spanish here then; it's mostly German or Japanese people who take over the hotels and campgrounds and revel in the tremendous heat.

Winter, however, is another story. Raw beauty abounds. The weather is magnificent. Snowstorms wail away in Denver and

Cincinnati and New York City, but at Ubehebe Crater, the Race-track, the Devil's Cornfield, and Artist's Drive the weather is fair and warm, with blue skies and magnificent vistas that compete for attention, and it's hard to take it all in.

After Death Valley we'll head down to the low deserts, stopping at the **Salton Sea**, before heading to the **Anza-Borrego**. We'll cross over to **Yuma**, and visit the Official Center of the World.

In each part of the book there's an *If You Go* section that tells how to get to the locations discussed. However, be aware that land use rules change and environmental policies can be whimsical. Powerful forces are working on both sides of the issue of public access to pub-

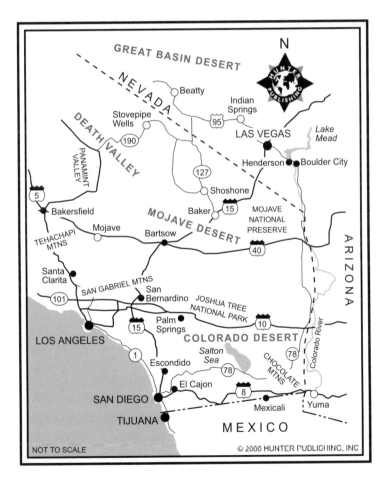

NOT TO SCALE © 2000 HUNTER PUBLICI IINC, INC

lic lands. So some of the places identified may no longer be open to access. But, if we're lucky, other locations may open that are now legally designated "wilderness."

Eco-Awareness

The legal designation of "wilderness" has closed tens of thousands of acres from public access by vehicle. This essentially forces people out of the wilderness land, and increases the vehicle use on non-wilderness land. Yes, we are allowed to hike in; but few of us do. Who's going to carry survival gear, water and cameras a dozen miles in desert heat, when we can use our wheels to head to another destination? So the bottom line is, while the "wilderness" is protected, the non-wilderness land is subjected to more damage from heavier use.

Land use has been a war fought on many fronts since the 1960s. The issues are very emotional; no one who lives, works or plays on the desert can be without strong feelings about them. There are as many sides in this war as there are warriors. This is public land and we all have a right to opinions on how it should be used. The hard-core greens radically oppose any use of the land except as a natural preserve, with no trace of humans anywhere. Developers and builders would have strip mines, solar power generation stations, prisons, and four-lane highways everywhere. Recreational users can't agree either. Some want to race dirt bikes and dune buggies up the hills and through the canyons; others want the damn noisy destructive things banned or, better yet, taken to the crusher and eliminated altogether. The greens, who should be an ally of responsible recreational users, hate four-wheeling and any mechanized activity; they want my Jeep in that crusher too. So we're not going to get along.

The Federal Bureau of Land Management (BLM) has been in the middle between these groups, trying to satisfy all of these constituents and making decisions that are radically stupid to some and eminently sensible to others. They are in a difficult position and haven't yet satisfied everyone. So the war goes on, and changes in land use policies occur with every election.

The BLM rules for desert adventuring on open land are summarized in the back of this book, along with a list of desert BLM offices and websites for additional information. With the exception of total prohibition of vehicles in Wilderness areas, the BLM's rules for visitors make sense and are easy to follow. For the most part they are simple and practical, involving not much more than common courtesy and being respectful of the environment and the rights of the others around you.

The Mojave

Introduction

Rich with folklore, laden with fables of gold, silver, minerals and gems – the Mojave sings in the hearts of Rainbow Chasers everywhere. Weekend prospectors still search its hills and valleys, betting on their one great chance to hit the big one. Beautiful desert scenery coupled with the romance of ghost towns and old mines make this one of the most fascinating areas of the Southwest.

Most of the Mojave is high desert, ranging from 1,000 to 5,000 feet in the flatlands to high mountain peaks of 10,000 feet or more. That makes the Mojave a little more tolerable in summer, as the temperatures don't usually hit the extreme highs of 120° or worse, as is experienced in Death Valley or the Anza-Borrego desert area. It also can snow here, though it won't remain on the ground for very long.

The Mojave begins north and east of Los Angeles, beyond the San Bernardino Mountains, and east of the Tehachapis. It's a 30-minute drive from the San Fernando Valley to Palmdale. The San Bernardinos are an effective barrier, keeping much of the pollution and a lot of the people from southern California away. It's only 30 minutes driving time, but it is a world apart from the Hollywood hills and freeway jangle of the greater LA basin.

Nobody – not geologists, cartographers, politicians, or the military (who owns huge areas of the desert) – seems to agree on the boundaries of the Mojave Desert. Southward, the Mojave merges into the Sonoran (Colorado) desert somewhere between Interstate Highway 40 and Interstate Highway 10. To the east, the Colorado River near Needles, and the Arizona city of Kingman, are adequate borders.

Northward, Death Valley and the grasslands north of Las Vegas mark the change to the Great Basin.

The Mojave covers thousands and thousands of square miles – as much as 25,000 square miles, if you extend the borders of the Mojave to the maximum. A good third of this area is under military control and can't be accessed by the general public. Other huge areas are federally administered as part of Death Valley National Park, the Mojave National Preserve, and Joshua Tree National Park. More land is officially designated as Wilderness or under state park control.

The California Desert Protection Act of 1994 set aside vast areas of the Mojave for preservation. This controversial legislation stopped development and off-road use of huge tracts of desert and created huge wilderness areas in which motor vehicles are prohibited. But it also set aside huge areas for exploration by vehicle, and preserved some of the most magnificent desert areas as public land forever. This act created the Mojave National Preserve and upgraded Death Valley and Joshua Tree to national park status. Limited travel and land use is allowed in these areas.

But much of the desert is BLM open land – administered by the Federal Bureau of Land Management – and as this is publicly owned land, people are free to come and go. We can rockhound, prospect for gold, hike, and let our spirits soar. Innumerable trails head off into the distance, with few restrictions. It is a vast area where we can still visit nature and rest our eyes on open spaces and bare land. There are some commonsense rules and restrictions that the BLM enforces, but a simple premise will keep any desert wanderer from running afoul of the law on BLM open land. Just follow the rules of treading lightly: leave nothing but tracks and (in the preserve and the national parks, as well as at any site of historical interest) take nothing but photographs.

The Essence of the Mojave

The central city of the California Mojave is **Barstow**. Major cities include the Antelope Valley cities of Palmdale/Lancaster/Quartz Hill in the southwestern corner of the desert; Victorville, Hesperia and Apple Valley south of Barstow; and Ridgecrest, to the north. Eastward are cities such as Las Vegas, Bullhead City and Needles on the Colorado River, and the Arizona town of Kingman, home of turquoise and copper.

Small towns with great character dot the map. **Boron** is home of not only a great rock shop, but also a nice museum and a couple of fine restaurants. **Randsburg** is a monument to the miners and Rainbow Seekers of the 1800s. Cantil, Ludlow and Baker, Mojave and Trona, Johannesburg and Red Mountain, all have their unique place in desert lore, and a visit to each town is an adventure.

For botanists, what separates the Mojave from other deserts is the **Joshua tree**. This unique fellow grows very slowly, often taking decades to reach the stature of a tree, and lives only on the Mojave. The unique combination of soil, annual rainfall, elevation, amount of sunlight, and so on led this very tall lily to claim only this piece of desert as its home. It's the symbol of the Mojave.

To geologists, the most unusual aspect of this desert is its lack of drainage. Many of the valleys do not drain. The dry arroyos simply end at a dry lakebed. Over the eons these lakebeds (called playas) became concentrated with minerals and alkalis, creating huge salt flats and deposits of borax that are now mined with huge open pit operations.

The **desert tortoise** is another benchmark of the Mojave. He's an unusual creature with a lifestyle that is particularly demanding and, frankly, unappealing. I admire him, but don't have any envy for his arduous life. His status (like so many things on the Mojave) is controversial. Some biologists believe that he's endangered, while others say his numbers are increasing. In fact, one theory holds that the desert tortoise exists in greater numbers now than 100 years ago, because his biggest enemy – man, in the form of Chemehuevis Indians who thought tortoises made a delicious dinner – no longer hunts him for food. Either way, this desert is his home, and he belongs here.

You'll see him only occasionally, slowly and calmly wandering the sands and clay. He's lucky to be alive. Born of parents who have abandoned him, his first four or five years are spent learning the ropes of desert survival on his own, without even a hard shell yet to protect him from the eagles, hawks and coyotes. He gets to eat only

Mojave Desert

in the spring and fall, when the wildflowers and desert grasses are tender and succulent. He stores up body fat and water, but he must get mighty hungry and thirsty during the long hot days of summer. If some tourist comes along and picks him up, he urinates all over himself, losing his valuable water supply – perhaps dying as a result. If he has a long wait for water, he may not make it.

But those that survive these hardships might live a hundred years. Some of the old tortoises walking the desert today might have watched a few of the original Rainbow Chasers become old men. The parents of these tortoises – while not model care-givers to their children – watched settlers endure the Mojave Trail while on their way to the promised land of California. Their parents saw the early Spanish explorers, and were dinner for the first Americans.

The desert tortoise is a good allegory for the desert. It is a place of slow change and he's survived through patience, endurance, and the flexibility to adapt to the harsh desert environment. In truth, he's done better than humans, with far less damage to the other inhabitants of his land.

Prickly Pear cactus, a desert dweller.

During the last half of the 1800s and into the start of the 20th century, the Mojave was a very busy place. For all its apparent emptiness and wild, undisturbed scenery, there probably isn't a place on this desert that a Rainbow Chaser did not see, not a likely-looking prospect anywhere that he didn't assess. The human population a hundred years ago was larger than it is now. The desert is the only area in California to actually decline in population since the big boom began in 1849. While this trend is reversing, the growth on the fringes of the Los Angeles metropolitan area and in the main population centers. Away from that influence, the desert is dotted with ghost towns and mining camps, railroad stations and army camps that are nearly all abandoned and are in the process of being reclaimed by the desert. The people are gone, but the cactus and creosote remain. As do the colors, the rocks, and the fascination.

The stories of these camps are rich and have grown into legendary folklore to the point that it's hard now – just a little over a hundred years later – to separate fact from fiction. It's part of the lure of the Mojave, to feel the excitement of its recent past while experiencing its eternal beauty. Those stories breathe life into this strange land.

If You Go

The Mojave is a wonderful place to visit, but come prepared. Much of the desert is empty and not patrolled. The appendix at the end of this book that discusses desert travel. Yes, it's just common sense, but read it over anyway; maybe you can improve upon my list of things to take and things to do. Drink your gallon of water a day.

One thing you should do is nothing.

Usually this "If You Go" section will contain practical advice. This time I'm waxing philosophic. Again: do absolutely nothing. It is the most important thing you can do for yourself. Stop and find some shade. That isn't easy, so you may have to make some. One of the many things I like about my Jeep Cherokee is the tailgate. Park in the right spot, with the sun at the hood, then put up the tailgate and there's a place to sit in the shade. Sit quietly and soak up the silence, watch the ants work away, feel the breeze as it sways the creosote. Above all, don't ponder work, problems at home or the hassles of your daily life. And don't even think of turning on the radio. Don't do anything.

After a while, a whole new world appears before you; it is the wonderful small world of the Mojave. The delicate plants. The tiny animals. The grains of sand, the deep, deep blue sky, and the passing light clouds. Maybe you'll hear a coyote in the distance, a friendly yipping. Study the ground; amazing things go on there.

Mojave Desert

Make a camp if you have to, but don't disturb our small friends and the delicate little plants. Stop and absorb the desert, let it absorb you, and it will bring peace to your soul. Life moves too fast as it is. When you go to the Mojave, I highly recommend that you make a point of stopping and doing nothing at all.

I do it every time I go.

Last Chance Canyon

Last Chance Canyon ranks high on my list of favorite spots on the Mojave. Wild and empty, the canyon tells you why Rainbow Chasers came to the desert, and why they stayed. It's in the El Paso Mountains, east of the Sierras and north of Mojave. Nearby is Randsburg. The canyon is now part of **Red Rock Canyon State Park**, which is headquartered a few miles west. The canyon certainly doesn't look like much from the highway on the flats. The El Pasos look like typical desert hills, a little more boring than most, with nothing much to commend them except some interesting place names: Burro Schmidt's Tunnel, Cudahy Camp and, of course, Last Chance itself.

But looks are deceiving. This is one of the most fascinating areas on this desert. Mining began here in the late 1800s. There's gold, and the Rainbow Chasers may have left some of it for today's desert wanderers; enough of us go looking for it that someone, somewhere ought to make another strike. But the gold we find here isn't just in the soil; it's in the canyon walls, the creosote bushes, and the desert tortoises. It's something you take home without removing a thing from the desert.

The canyon starts out innocently enough, from the Redrock-Randsburg Road south of the El Pasos. Heading up the rock fan – called a *bajada* – a cut in the mountains slowly reveals itself, forming the canyon. The trail follows a sandy wash and there's not even a need for four-wheel-drive.

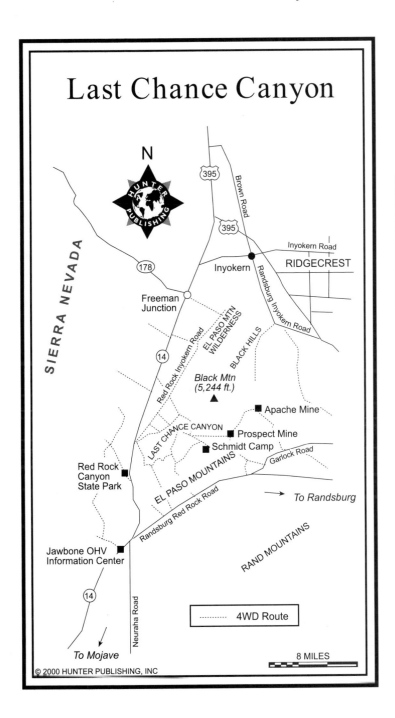

Last Chance Canyon

No need, that is, until you turn the first couple of bends and the rocks start in earnest. Then the canyon walls narrow, and 12 feet above ground level you see the markings of a flood: water-washed walls, sticks and branches caught in the brush and brown rocks at the flood line. The canyon is a rockhound's dream. There's agate, jasper, chalcedony, and more; fossils and shells from the time this land was the floor of a prehistoric ocean. Trace amounts of gold – mostly in flakes, but an occasional nugget – have been found here.

Desert history books tell us that this canyon was first prospected by the '49ers who didn't strike it rich in the big gold rush – or during the silver and gold rush to Comstock and the Washoe 10 years later in Nevada. These prospectors, few of whom did more than scratch out a bare living, became known as Rainbow Chasers. They were men who kept following the lure of the big strike, wandering from "excitement" to "excitement," down from Reno and Virginia City through Bishop, Bodie, Lone Pine, and Death Valley. The ones who kept coming eventually came here, to the Mojave Desert. In the 1890s some of them struck it rich in nearby Randsburg, Goler, Garlock, and a dozen other places. Most of them didn't, and they found themselves running out of land to explore. All the good land had been panned and dug, with the claims filed and the mills operating on the successful sites. That's why they called this Last Chance Canyon. It was their last chance to hit the big one.

You still see their diggings here in Last Chance. There are also diggings from the hard times of the '30s, when more modern Rainbow Chasers came to find opportunity. Up until the time the canyon became part of Red Rock State Park in the mid-1990s, people still dug for gold here.

After you pass those diggings, you're on a serious four-wheel-drive trail. We wound through the canyon, taking an hour to travel the three miles to **Cudahy Camp**, on a rock trail that must change with every storm. There's a point where a tan sandstone cliff looms on the left, and Jeep-size boulders lie on the dry riverbottom. Recently fallen Jeep-size boulders. Maybe even tank-size boulders. Boulders that are much bigger than the little dinky Jeeps we drive today.

The cliff doesn't look stable, either.

It's a little too easy to visualize another one of those tan sandstone cliff faces deciding to come down to the bottom of the canyon. Sometimes it's not good to be blessed with an active imagination.

In times like these, you think of avalanches. It's sound that activates them, right? You see it in all the movies – a loud bang, a roar, and a mountain of snow buries the cabin and the trees and a skier or two. It's too easy to see the same thing happening here, an avalanche of sandstone burying the Jeep, Suz, and me forever.

They call it exfoliation. It's a harmless-sounding term. But if that cliff chooses to exfoliate while we're under it, you won't be able to finish reading this book because I won't be around to write it.

Beyond the cliff and the fallen boulders, it doesn't get any easier to go through. The trail winds around boulders, touches the cliff face, wandering like a path through a teenager's bedroom. We have no choice; I put the Jeep in gear and we drive through, the trail's pucker factor easing at the end of the obstacle course where we emerged unharmed.

As the canyon widens, a new vista opens up, one of multiple colors and shapes. Water flows in the creek bed, a narrow stream easily forded, an alkali-rich flow that leaves the sand stained white. Salt cedar – reedy plants that are too tall to call bushes and too short to call trees – line the water. There are signs of wildlife: tracks of deer, a horse or two, a wildcat, foxes and coyotes. To the west is **Roaring Ridge**, a barren piece of work where nothing grows because the wind won't let it. To the east are **Black Mountain** and the hills of the **El Pasos**.

The hills show the unique geography of the area. Some of them are capped with the black and brown of lava, from an eruption that cut loose long ago and far away. Below the lava are sandstone bluffs, red or gray or brown, depending upon the light and the minerals contained in the hill. There are pink cliffs, made of delicate sandstone that is continually being carved by the winds.

There are yellow and white stains, too, that are man-made. Old mines scar the mountainsides. The old Dutch Boy Cleanser open pit dug out thousands of tons of material used to clean homes around the world. It left a mountain changed and scarred forever, in beautiful colors perhaps, but gone are the plants and animals, the thin topsoil, the network of creosote bushes that made the desert a viable home to its inhabitants.

A terrible dilemma, this. Do we continue to dig the minerals and metals of the earth, at the price of the flora and fauna? The impact of past mining operations is incredible. Acres and acres of soil are ripped up, and the unwanted waste is dumped on still more acres of land. Minerals, acids, and alkalis leach out of the dumps and contaminate much more of the surrounding countryside. Mud and silt, as well as the leachates, are carried downstream, further modifying the environment in immeasurable ways and in far away places.

Or do we do without these things, stifle the growth of industry and development, for the sake of a few rattlesnakes and jackrabbits?

The mining goes on today, but with some controls to reduce the damage done at areas away from the mine. The world's largest open pit mine is a few miles away, north of Boron, where huge trucks cart out borates and giant mills reduce it to usable form. Near Randsburg, a man-made mountain of mined rock and soil is washed with cyanide to extract gold. Down on the dry lakebeds, salt is dug and shipped to tables across the land.

Environmentalists say we should put a stop to all this destruction. Industry says they are doing their part to minimize environmental damage, and will reclaim the land after they are done. The people that live here say they need the jobs, and there's plenty of desert to go around.

My desert-dancing partner Suz says let's load up and get on down the canyon; the light's going to fade soon and we have more desert to explore.

The road opens up now, following the still-wet riverbed around a bend past the Cudahy mine. To the left is Roaring Ridge. We climb it – not easy, with Suz very uncomfortable. We're on a narrow ridge with steep dropoffs on both sides and the wind is blowing. It always does here. But the view is stupendous. There's jasper and agate, nice material that would polish up well. We left it for the next desert dancers who'll come along and find this place.

If You Go

Located in the El Paso Mountains, near the Red Rock State Park headquarters, Last Chance Canyon is one of the most scenic and awesome desert trails on the western Mojave. From the south, the trail ranks as one of the most rugged canyon climbs in the desert. I took this trail in a Cherokee Laredo that had been lifted three inches and has great low-range gears; in any less-capable vehicle I probably would have turned around. Any vehicle that is larger or has less ground clearance is at risk for body damage. From the north is a trail that most two-wheel-drive vehicles could take, although it does have some patches of sand. It leads you into the main valley.

Be aware there are no services anywhere in the canyon – no stores, gas stations, or restaurants. In fact, there are seldom many people; perhaps a few working at the Cudahy mine, and that's it. You are on your own here. If you're not familiar with desert travel, read the section on desert travel in the Appendix *before venturing out. Supplies are available at the Jawbone Canyon store south of Red Rock State Park on Highway 14, or in Randsburg (to the east), California City (to the south), or Inyokern (north on 14).*

Camping is available at **Red Rock Canyon State Park,** ☎ *(661) 942-0662, or anywhere on BLM land. See the* Appendix *for more information.*

Exploring Last Chance Canyon
from the South

The southern trail begins on the Redrock-Randsburg road 5.6 miles east of its intersection with Highway 14. The GPS coordinates are N35° 21.672', W117° 53.943. You'll proceed north, and enter the canyon about a mile up the trail.

This part of Last Chance Canyon – from the canyon entrance to a point two or three miles into the mountains – is now under the con trol of Red Rock State Park. Be aware that there is talk of shutting off canyon access with a locked gate. (If it ever happens, feel free to join me in a letter-writing campaign to re-open the trail.)

The canyon trail gets real exciting. Numerous rock hazards make this trip very difficult, and in a few places you'll be next to sandstone cliffs that "exfoliate" a little too often for comfort. The Jeep-size boulders that have bounded down the cliffs make this a place where you really don't want to hang out too long. But, off to the right and left, magnificent vistas of colorful cliffs and rock outcroppings make the trip worthwhile.

At about four miles from the pavement you will encounter a small stream that often has a little water, and the **Cudahy Camp**. To your left is **Roaring Ridge**, a place where the wind doesn't seem to ever stop.

Here, the canyon trail widens, and access is easy. At eight miles from pavement, there'll be an intersection with a signpost. Bear left to go to Highway 14 – you'll come out at **Hart's Place**, a total of 15 miles from where you left the pavement. By turning right at the signpost, however, you will get to **Burro Schmidt's Tunnel**. This is an easy wheel. The Schmidt camp is at GPS coordinates N35° 24.673', W117° 52.062', and there are signs along the way for directions.

Exploring Last Chance Canyon from the North

At the intersection of Highway 14 and the Redrock-Randsburg Road, proceed north on 14 through Red Rock State Park. About five miles beyond the park you'll come to **Hart's Place**, which is just a few buildings on the west side of the road. There's a small sign for **Burro Schmidt's Tunnel** that points you toward a good, wide dirt road on the right (east) side. Follow this road into the canyon. You'll come to the intersection and signpost after a few miles.

Most of the roads here are adequately maintained for two-wheel-drive vehicles. However, such vehicles should stay on the main, graded roads and watch for sand patches. Don't stop if you enter a sand patch; keep going until you're clear of it.

Golden Valley

O ur expedition to the Golden Valley wilderness began on a fine spring day, the sort of day that promises to last forever and lets the desert cacti forget about heat and dust. We were hunting petroglyphs.

There are petroglyphs on the desert, well-preserved artifacts of ancient man's artwork that tell the stories of hunts gone good or bad, of drought and rain, of the things that are real and basic. The Spanish, 19th-century prospectors, bandits, common travelers, and 20th-century hooligans also left petroglyphs of a different sort, usually hand-carved into rock faces. These are messages that tell stories of gold and silver mines, stashes from trips made long ago, or perhaps just the markings of someone who wanted to tell the world he had been there.

These glorious messages from the past are hard to find. We had directions to some that were on a cliff face in the Lava Mountains, west of Golden Valley. We'd also been told about a particularly fine outcropping of opalite, on the eastern edge of the Lavas. These were our targets for the day.

To get there we proceeded north from Johannesburg on the Trona Road. Steam Well Road takes off a mile or so past the intersection of Highway 395 and Trona Road. It skims around the north edge of Red Mountain, with the Lava Mountains showing themselves to the north.

Magnificent patches of desert wildflowers were painting the landscape in glorious hues of yellow, purple, red and blue. It was the spring of El Niño, when unusual rains brought thundering walls of water through the arroyos, leaving in its path the most water the desert had seen in decades. The trail – normally driveable by someone careful and courageous in a family car – was a rough one, thanks to these storms, as the gully crossings were often deep and fresh washouts. They called for some careful and slow work, even in my tall Jeep with its trail tires.

It's thrilling to watch a desert thunderstorm – thrilling, but harrowing. You never quite know what will happen. These storms can come up quickly. There's a blast of wind, laden with dust and grit, sandblasting your face and your windshield, then lightning and thunder so powerful it rattles your bones and booms through your head. Then comes the rain, falling with the force of bullets. If you are lucky enough to be in your car when it hits, the pounding of the rain on the roof drowns out any chance of conversation and the sheets of water keep you from seeing what's going on outside – though the thunderous roar makes you want to know. Then the flood comes down the canyons, a roiling brown mud mess, carrying creosote branches and mesquite, a snake or two, plus any other unfortunates who got in the way. Pure primeval excitement.

You can see the marks from these storms along the access road to Golden Valley. The road passes to the east of **Red Mountain**, and there are the marks of yet another force that continually changes the face of the desert: the prospector.

In the late 1800s the Mojave swarmed with people. These guys – and quite a few women – came out here without four-wheel-drive vehicles, radios, GPS, cell phones, Jerry cans and other modern conveniences; no motor homes, travel trailers, or microwaveable TV dinners made their lives easier. They came on foot, on burros, on horseback, and by stagecoach to hunt for wealth.

Some of them made it big. In Randsburg, the **Rand discovery** (later called the Yellow Aster) became a huge success, and was one of the few gold mines that actually made its founders wealthy. Most of the time, a gold mine would be developed by someone who had bought the claim from the original prospector, who didn't usually have enough money to invest in the tools and equipment, plus the manpower, to make the mine pay off.

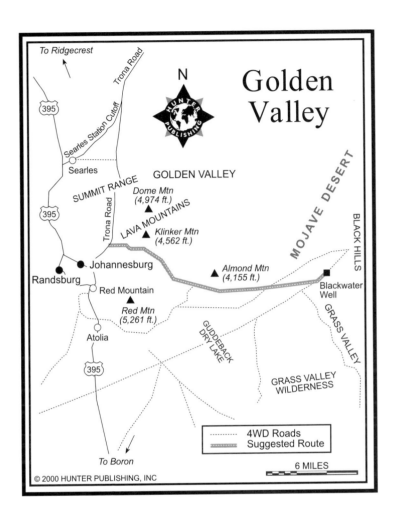

Mojave Desert

The Rainbow Chaser

Here, on both sides of our trail to Golden Valley, you see the signs of prospecting, both old and new. There are diggings to the south of the trail, on a ridge that falls away from Red Mountain. These diggings are enticing. Did a bearded, wandering Rainbow Chaser, his face lined and chiseled and sun dark, lead his burro up this draw, following some promising float till he came to a ledge that smelled of gold?

Can't you just see him? His Levis are faded almost to white, his cotton shirt dirty and dark with sweat. A gray flop hat covers his stringy hair, his blue eyes sparkle with excitement as he examines a piece of quartz that looks good. The quartz is lined with a black trace and something that glitters just a tiny bit. He sets his pickax down, pulls his pack off the back of the mule, makes a dry camp and sets up to do a little chasin' of his rainbow. With his shovel he mucks out some overburden, and dry-pans the black sand that settled in the cracks of the rock. With his pick he pulls out rock, breaks it up and, finally, there! A tiny nugget of gold, gleaming bright and pretty as can be, a month's wages in his hands.

Could this be it – the next big find?

It's not placer gold. Placer is rounded and smooth, tumbled and beaten as it is washed downstream. This is lode gold, rough and sharp and there has to be more of it, more than this tiny nugget. Gold likes to be with others of its kind. If there's one nugget, one sharp piece of lode gold, maybe there is more, surely there is more, and the mother lode – the source of this piece – can't be far away. Our prospector works feverishly now, searching for more nuggets.

When he finds more, a big beautiful nugget laced in a piece of quartz, he stops, and decides this is the place. It still might just be 'float' – a rock that was broken off and carried away by water, wind, an animal, or a human in ancient times – but he doesn't think so. This is too good. His heart is pounding, his hands are shaking, and dreams are building in his head. He stashes the finds in his poke then builds his monument, a rock cairn. In a tin can he places his claim, written on a dirty, torn piece of paper, and on the four corners of his claim he builds stone monuments to mark its borders.

He's got his "location." It's 20 acres on which he just might find his fortune, and just a few days to trace the ore and make the adjustments to the boundary that assures he keeps the heart of the deposit to himself. For as sure as it is hot on a summer day, the secret of gold will leak out. Word of his find is already traveling on the wind, and he'll soon have plenty of company. Feverishly he stakes out a few more claims in the names of his grubstakers.

A year's wages, right in his poke. He pulls it out and looks at it, making sure he isn't heat-sick or crazy. He puts it under a rock for safekeeping, but can't stand to be away from it.

The next few days are the days he's dreamed of, our Rainbow Chaser, as he works in earnest on his claim. He wakes early, to the sound of coyotes and the bright of first light, and he fries up a few biscuits and beans for breakfast. He grabs his pick and shovel and keeps working the claim, separating the promising rock from the waste. It's good, it's rich, it's the rock he's always dreamed of: chunks of gold-bearing quartz, beautifully laced and lined with it, and sometimes a big nugget. He works the rock down, separating out the gold-bearing ore, dreaming of his big moment when he'll ride into town, step into the saloon and tell the boys what he's found. He'll buy a round – hell, he'll buy the bar! And there'll be a celebration the likes of which they've never seen.

Then the stampede. The boys won't leave him alone. A few pump him for what he'll tell about where he made the strike, and he'll tease them along, and some will slip away to backtrack him to the claim. They'll find it, too, eventually; a secret like this can't be kept, no sir. And after a glorious festival, a real hoop-ti-do celebration, he'll lead them back to his mine so the boys can file their own prospects and share in the wealth.

Then the town grows. A tent city will spring up first, as the boys will have nothing on their minds but finding the gold. There'll be a saloon, not just for the relief and relaxation that the alcohol brings, but because saloons were the social halls and meeting places of the time. Somebody will start a restaurant for the miners who are too busy to cook for themselves, and there'll be a Chinese laundry and a general store. All these will spring up within days, and this peaceful, empty desert will be a beehive of activity.

So when our Rainbow Chaser has a fair amount of color he loads up the burro and heads to town, and then the whole cycle plays out, just as it did dozens of times, whenever a new strike was found. Sometimes the boys would go on a toot that lasted for weeks. When they came out of it, with no gold nuggets or even any dust left for supplies, the desert would have pulled a dirty trick and wiped out any trace of the trail. It would have washed the hills clean and changed

Mojave Desert

things so much that his booze-befuddled brain couldn't tell him how to find his way back to the claim. It would drive the boys nuts, much less our Rainbow Chaser, trying to find that lost mine. Years would be spent hunting for it, and the campfire legends would grow.

Or, our prospector could stay out so long that he'd use up all his supplies and not make it back to town. He'd die on the way, the location of his mine dying with him. He'd be found someday, with his gold dust and nuggets, and another story of lost riches would be born.

More often, what would happen is what appears to have happened here. First the hoop-ti-do party, then a rush back to the claim. An overnight sensation would bring hundreds of stampeders and the desert would fill with claims, the sounds of shoveling and picking and shouting filling the air. Exuberant mine camps would spring up and roar their way through the nights, the saloons and honkytonks taking the gold the miners would dig by day.

But only a few lucky ones would find any gold at all. Hundreds would chase the excitement, but it would pay off only for a few. There'd be a little placer gold, a few dozen nuggets and a few tons of black sand to refine, then the gold would peter out and the camp would die. Eventually, another Rainbow Chaser would rush into the saloon, shout his Eureka, and another stampede would empty the town. The tents would come down, the ladies would load into the wagons, and another mining town would be born.

It wasn't just the gold that drove them. It was the excitement, and the life. The hunt for gold on the desert kept these men out till a certain wildness overcame them, and only the stillness of the desert calmed their souls.

Their signature on the land remains in a few mine shafts, random piles of overburden, and an occasional stone hut that has withstood the desert storms. Golden Valley is empty now, preserved by Government order as a wilderness with limited access, thanks to the political action of the environmentalists.

We couldn't get to the petroglyphs, nor to the opalite cliff. The trail to them was blocked off and a sign threatened serious consequences if we dared to proceed. Where men used to wander freely is now inaccessible. Our desert dancing trip ended near the locked gate for the

Naval target range, where multimillion-dollar jets blow hell out of the sand and creosote that isn't protected.

If You Go

Highway 395 intersects the Trona Road between Red Mountain and Johannesburg. Proceed northward on the Trona Road about 1.4 miles, and turn eastward on Steam Well Road (unpaved). Red Mountain will be to the south, and the Lava Mountains to the north. About two miles from the pavement will be a road heading northward, blocked by rocks and BLM warning signs. The petroglyphs are reported to be down this road about two miles.

Farther down Steam Well Road, as you drop into the long valley, you'll see diggings and exploratory mine workings on both sides of the road. Remember that land on the north side of the road is legally designated as "Wilderness" and vehicle access, or prospecting, is not allowed.

Boron to Randsburg

History

In the mid-1800s, the Rand Mountains had yet to be named. They'd been scouted some, but it took three last-chance Rainbow Chasers – John Singleton, F. M. Mooers, and Charlie Burcham – until the early 1890s to discover that one of the peaks in this small mountain range was a mountain of gold.

These three prospectors were really down on their luck. They barely had enough beans to last while they established their claim, and virtually each day they used the gold they found to finance another day's digging. They were about to sell their claim to a developer when Rose Burcham, the wife of one of the prospectors, arrived and saved the day – and their fortune. She wouldn't allow the sale, and found a way to finance the mine's development.

To her husband and his associates, this was a woman who was worth far more than her weight in gold. The Yellow Aster became one of the biggest gold mines on the Mojave.

The prospectors called their discovery the Rand, and the town that sprang up became Randsburg. The mountains they were in became the Rand Mountains, and the boys changed the name of the mine to the Yellow Aster. The town and the area boomed. Soon over 2,500 people inhabited Randsburg and it was a beehive of activity. Gold mines blossomed on the hillsides and the boom was on.

The boom faded, as they do around here; but the town would not die. Today, a few hundred hardy souls remain and keep the spirit of Randsburg alive. The town survives off a little mining, and a little tourism, as do the nearby communities of Red Mountain and Johannesburg.

Randsburg Today

The heart of the town hasn't changed much since the first solid buildings went up. It's a little desert community built on the side of the mountains, a few strings of false-fronted buildings, lackadaisical sidewalks, and collages of old cars, trucks, mining equipment, and stuff that in other places might be called junk. But here, it establishes character, so it can't be bad.

The general store has a long counter and malt machines from the 1930s. There's a rack with treasure maps, books on hunting gold, and locally produced histories, all great reading. There are a couple of saloons still operating here. As it was in the old days, here in Randsburg a good saloon is a lot more than a watering hole; it's the heart of a community and a meeting place where business gets done, as well as socializing and problem-solving. The White House sits on the main drag, across from The Joint.

The Joint is a Randsburg landmark. Olga – who stands maybe five feet tall – has run the place since the 1950s, and she's still working, while her son has retired from a government job in Visalia. She opened The Joint with her husband, who died in 1957. They say the jukebox quit when the husband died, and hasn't worked since, but don't believe it. Another story says that Olga hates loud music and she just made sure the jukebox didn't ever work again. She started the story so no well-meaning customer would try to fix it for her.

The Joint has an old rock wall for a front, backed by whitewashed clapboard, and an old, old neon sign hanging from the false front. Inside, there are no pretensions; it's just a bar, a few tables and a wooden floor that echoes every footstep. The old jukebox is on the right, lifeless. Along the wall are maps to rockhound sites and gold mines, as well as pictures and newspaper clippings from better days. Olga works behind the bar that stretches along the left wall. It is dark, and cool, and the restrooms are down a tiny hall in the very back of the long, narrow building.

Olga is a quiet, shy, and careful woman. She'll wait and see what you're made of before she'll start talking to you much. She's been known to close the bar when rowdy bikers come to town; to quietly lock the door, escort her customers out, and close for the day rather than put up with the noise and fuss. But if you're the friendly sort, or just sit quietly and mind your own business, it isn't long before her curiosity and good manners overcome her reticence and she starts talking away. Soon, you know the current events in Randsburg; how the environmental laws make mining all but impossible these days, and how little help Washington or Sacramento is, and how much trouble the bureaucrats and lawmakers cause these people who just want to be left alone to do their own thing.

Mining is still the number one topic in Randsburg. Not just gold; many locals work at the 20 Mule Team Borax mine in Boron, or at the salt flats, or other locales nearby. Some still prospect, searching out the earth's treasures just as did the founders of this community. Even Olga isn't immune to the call of gold. She's in partnership with some friends who have a claim they are developing.

Tourists are the number two topic. It seems everyone wants them, but not the troubles they bring, and not the tourists who think the desert and little burgs like this are places to raise hell and not pay the price. Stories abound of Los Angeles types who think the law stops at the LA county line. Particularly bad, according to a local who joined in the conversation, was an LA cop who finally got to know

Mojave Desert

the inside of a Kern County jail as well as he knew his own patrol car back home.

Randsburg is a fun place, one of our favorites to visit. You can get to Randsburg on paved roads, from either Highway 395 or State Route 14. But that's the easy way.

Cross-Country to Randsburg

Another route to Randsburg is to head straight north from Boron, driving about 25 miles across the desert, then climbing the Rand Mountains, looking over the mines, and dropping down into Randsburg. The last few miles are a four-wheel low-range expedition worthy of any desert dancer.

That's the way I like to go. We don't always get to go that way, because Suz likes to actually get there, and a cold brew in the cool recesses of The Joint beckons mightily on a hot summer day.

When we go this way, we take off from the central exit in Boron along Route 58. Boron houses one of the desert's fast-fading institutions: the **Desert Discoveries Rock Shop**.

Rock shops used to be almost as common as gas stations, located at empty crossroads or at the edge of town, serving as trading posts and information centers. They'd have agates and hollow geodes, petrified wood and maybe a dinosaur footprint or two. You'd pull up to an old building – maybe, like the shop in Boron, a World War II vintage quonset hut, or a stone and wood shack that was neglected. It looked a little forlorn because if the owner wasn't busy tending customers, he was either cutting and polishing rocks or out hunting for more raw material. He darn sure wasn't wasting his time fixing up a yard or painting a building.

There'd be an old Jeep Wagoneer around, or maybe an ancient Dodge Power Wagon, dented and dirty but not a speck of rust, with tough-looking tires and faded paint. It would be in great mechanical condition, but ancient, and not a bit economical or easy to drive. That doesn't matter; what does matter is its ability to get to the outcroppings and haul back enough rock to keep its owner busy cutting and polishing till the next time he had the urge to head out.

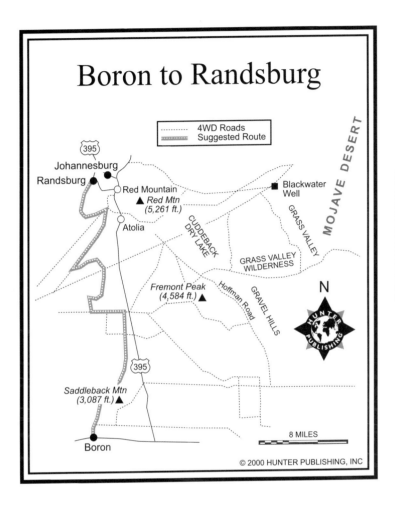

Boron to Randsburg

- · · · · · · · 4WD Roads
- ▨▨▨▨▨ Suggested Route

MOJAVE DESERT

395

Johannesburg
Randsburg ●
Red Mountain ○
▲ Red Mtn
(5,261 ft.)
Atolia ○

CUDDEBACK DRY LAKE

Blackwater ■
Well

GRASS VALLEY

GRASS VALLEY
WILDERNESS

Fremont Peak
(4,584 ft.) ▲

Hoffman Road

GRAVEL HILLS

N

HUNTER PUBLISHING

395

Saddleback Mtn
(3,087 ft.) ▲

8 MILES

Boron ●

© 2000 HUNTER PUBLISHING, INC

Mojave Desert

People don't seem to like rocks as much as they used to; rock shops are a dying business, and the Desert Discoveries shop is the only one for miles. It's a good one, too, with fine specimens from around the world, as well as from the Mojave. There's lots of quartz, in many varieties; tiger's eye, with beautiful bands of brown and black; TV rock, polished jasper, turquoise and jade; dozens and dozens of other varieties, polished or rough, small and large. It's a geological feast.

After an obligatory stop at the rock shop, and equally obligatory purchases of specimens that usually lose themselves in the car, we find ourselves heading north from Boron on a trail that initially is easily navigated in almost any vehicle. We pass over some small hills. East and north is a federal prison, a good place to keep crooked politicians out of sight, out of mind, away from the TV cameras and news media. East and south, near Kramer Junction, a huge bed of solar energy collectors convert the endlessly bright sunshine into electricity. South is Edwards Air Force Base, one of many military areas that take away huge chunks of desert from public access. West is a resort, with many trees, a golf course, horse trails, and luxury condos. Also off to the west are several subdivisions, most of them empty, except for the marked and platted roads.

No, this part of the desert isn't empty. You don't see all this activity from our trail, but once in a while you hear it, in the form of a jet fighter or experimental airplane being tested at Edwards or dropping a payload at China Lake. Thank goodness, there's enough room for all this activity, and still enough room for people like me to find empty trails.

A few miles north of Boron we cross the **20 Mule Team Road**. This is the trail that huge, overloaded wagons used to haul borates from Death Valley to the railhead in Mojave; a long – 200 mile long – dry, hot journey.

Past the trail, the road rises toward the Rand Mountains. At this elevation some grass grows with the desert shrub, and many a sheep spends the winter here. There are a few sheepherders' camps and watering holes as we make the long climb up to the Rands.

Soon we enter a forest of Joshua trees. These are old and imperturbable, some as high as 20 feet; real ancient guardians, standing watch over the valley and the hillsides.

But it's a complicated hunt for the right trail. The Bureau of Land Management has closed off many of the trails in the Rand Mountains to protect the environment, and the darn roads keep changing. We wander along, edging westward and north, and finally creep up a long canyon. The temperature gauge climbs, the air conditioner gets turned off, and when we stop for a rest and to let the Jeep cool, the air is so still you think you hear a coyote panting in the next canyon over.

There are diggings here, along the canyon, in the colorful rock faces, where Rainbow Chasers followed the boys who discovered the Rand was a rich, rich area. A few made it big. Most didn't, but they left their mark on the land before moving on to the next excitement.

Kangaroo Rats & Other Wildlife

Humans make big holes in the ground; dozens of smaller animals make small diggings. These miniature subterranean passages crumble beneath our feet when we get out of the Jeep and walk through the creosote to the dry riverbed that has spent centuries forming this canyon. The subterranean passages are home to an incredible number of animals. Many, if not most, of the small creatures of the desert adapt to summer heat by spending their days below ground.

The best known of these is probably the **kangaroo rat**, known to the biologists as *Dipodomys*. He's an odd fellow. He's a rodent, all right, but not really a rat, nor a marsupial. Silky-furred, compact, rather dainty, he's not at all ugly even if his head is almost as big as his body and his tail much longer than the rest of him put together. And is he fast: he takes off with bounding leaps, like a kangaroo, as fast as a bullet. Another of his amazing feats is that this fellow can live his whole life without a drop of water. All he needs is a little green food once in a while. He can even do without that, for his body is an astonishing chemistry kit that can synthesize water from starchy foods or fats.

This is a kangaroo rat's den we've inadvertently damaged. His sign is by the several entrances to his underground mansion. His tracks are easy to distinguish; there are the parallel marks of the two long-soled hind feet, and the curving, shallow furrow left by his long tail. Our few steps have crushed several square inches of underground passageways. He will have them fixed in no time, but we still cringe in guilt and try to walk around his home.

The kangaroo rat isn't the only desert dweller to spend the daylight hours underground. There are so many species of wild mice, and their numbers are so plentiful, that desert biologist Edmund Jaeger says "... there is scarcely a square foot of either brush-covered land, open desert, or rocky hillside that is not visited almost nightly by

Mojave Desert

these diligent harvesters as they search for food." The tracks of deer mice, pocket mice, grasshopper mice, and harvest mice are common enough to back up Jaeger's claim.

Back in the Jeep, its engine cooled somewhat, we start up the grade and top out beside the Yellow Aster mine. This man-created hole in the ground is not nearly as creative or charming as our kangaroo rat's was. Randsburg lies below us, a scattered collection of small buildings and mining tools. Beyond it are the El Paso Mountains, across a long hot valley that shimmers in the desert heat. The Joint beckons with a tall bottle of cold refreshment awaiting.

Yes, you can get to Randsburg on pavement. Just go up either 395 from Kramer Junction, or 14 from Mojave, and follow the signs. But why do that? Getting there by way of a four-wheel-drive trail puts me in the right frame of mind for visiting this wonderful old town, and makes that cold beer a welcome reward. The conversations with modern day Rainbow Chasers and Desert Dancers become a little more meaningful; I've earned a right to join them.

If You Go

Randsburg is a very charming little town, and if you find yourself anywhere near it, go. Much of it is closed on the weekdays, however. The general store and The Joint are usually open through the week, but not much else. It's still worth the trip. On the weekends, antique shops and a neat little museum are usually open.

Randsburg is not on a major highway. Even if it were, it's so small that if you blinked while racing by you'd miss it. So take your time. Head north on 395 from Kramer Junction, and watch for the signs as you pass through Johannesburg. The road takes off to the west and cuts through the Rand Mountains.

From Highway 14, the Redrock-Randsburg Road heads east from just south of Red Rock State Park. The road follows the El Paso Mountains. Near Garlock, at a well-marked intersection, you'll cut south into the Rand Mountains and the town of Randsburg.

Ridgecrest & Points North

About 25 miles north of Randsburg is a town that was almost known as Rattlesnake Gulch, back when it was born during World War II. There is some cattle and sheep ranching around, as well as some mining, but the town's main purpose then and now was to support the sprawling, desert-eating China Lake Naval Weapons Center. Fortunately for future Chamber of Commerce members and other local boosters, the name of Ridgecrest won out over Rattlesnake Gulch and other colorful choices – by one vote – when the citizens chose their town's name.

Since this is a military town, as goes the Navy budget, so goes Ridgecrest. China Lake sprawls northward for 40 miles from the town, with its flight line, repair centers, and target cities that exist for warriors to sharpen their flying and bombing skills. There is much less activity here than there was during the Cold War years, but a fine and modern town remains, and it's an excellent headquarters for off-highway adventures in the northern Mojave. There are several inexpensive motels, great restaurants, and a good resource center: the **Matarango Museum**.

Wild Horses

Another important resource near Ridgecrest is the **Regional Wild Horse & Burro Corrals**. Operated by the Bureau of Land Management, these corrals are the temporary home of the horses and burros caught in the Southwestern deserts and who are on their way to domestication. Over 1,000 horses and burros pass through these corrals each year.

Wild horses and burros are a tremendous problem throughout the desert Southwest. They aren't native to the desert regions; the horses date back to the time of the Spanish occupation of the Southwest,

Mojave Desert

and many of the burros are the descendants of those left behind by our Rainbow-Chasing prospectors. The animals have few effective predators, and the herds have grown to the point that they are an environmental disaster in some areas. So the BLM has developed a management program to capture and make them available for private adoption through the corrals. Wranglers from Ridgecrest are sent on roundups throughout the west to collect horses and burros in areas where the populations have become a problem.

While the heartbeat of Ridgecrest is closely tied to modern war machines, it is located in the center of the eastern Sierra mining country. Northeast is Trona, The Panamints and Death Valley. Northwest is Darwin, Cerro Gordo and, far to the north, Bodie – possibly the best-preserved ghost town in the West.

Trona Pinnacles.

Cerro Gordo

Cerro Gordo was discovered in 1865 in the tall Inyo Mountains, on the eastern side of Owens Lake. Pablo Floras found the strike, at the 8,500-foot level, and worked it quietly for two years. The mining operation was plagued with the traditional prospector's shortage – lack of development capital – and its success was limited. But in 1867 word leaked out that Buena Vista Peak was loaded with rich silver ore. The rush was on, and prospectors stormed the area to stake claims and make their fortunes.

One of the first on the scene was a shrewd operator: Victor Beaudry. He knew how to get the capital, and San Francisco money came to town as well as a mining engineer by the name of M.W. Belshaw. Belshaw moved quickly to secure control of the mining interests. He also piped in a reliable water supply, built the town's only smelter, and constructed the only road in or out of the Cerro Gordo. Belshaw and Beaudry quickly became partners, and the pair dominated business here and elsewhere on the desert for many years.

It was a very rich find. Cerro Gordo eventually was the richest silver mine ever found in California, producing some 2,200 tons of silver, lead, and zinc a year. The town, perched high up a canyon in some of the steepest mountains on the face of the earth, was one of the wildest, with a reputation for meanness and violence that was bested only by Bodie a few years later.

Rich it was but, like most of our remote mining towns, Cerro Gordo's existence was short-lived. The silver supply began to run out. In 1876 the smelter shut down and the town was virtually deserted by 1879, although several efforts have been made over the years to find a new fortune in Buena Vista Peak. Today, a bed and breakfast hotel and a few old buildings remain ready for visitors. The view from Cerro Gordo across Owens Valley to the Sierras is spectacular.

The transitory nature of the desert mining camps is obvious only when we look back over their short history. This period of discovery – from about 1850 till around 1915 – was intense and exciting, with fortunes waiting on the side of every mountain. There was no reason to think it would ever end.

But it did. The mines played out. The miners, suppliers, camp followers, and prostitutes (known as "soiled doves") knew that when the mines were done the paydays were gone and it was time to move on. From Washoe to Cerro Gordo, Darwin to Bodie, Panamint City to Rhyolite, they followed the prospectors who made the big strikes, and built ways to convert the output of the mines into spendable cash – in their pockets. In tracing the histories of these cities you'll see the

Mojave Desert

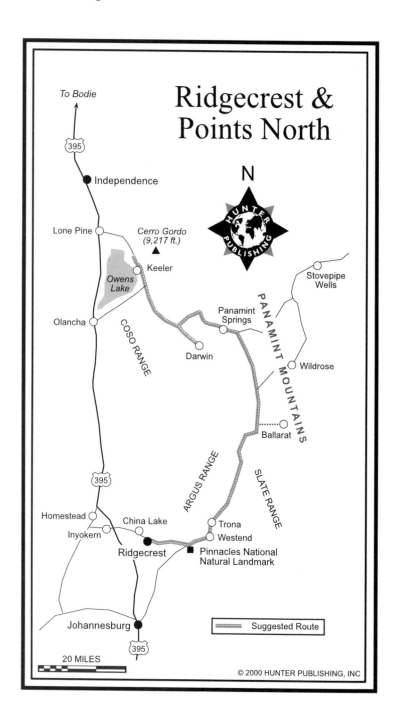

Ridgecrest & Points North

N

To Bodie

395

Independence

Lone Pine

Cerro Gordo
(9,217 ft.)

Keeler

Owens
Lake

Stovepipe
Wells

Panamint
Springs

Olancha

COSO RANGE

Darwin

PANAMINT MOUNTAINS

Wildrose

Ballarat

395

ARGUS RANGE

SLATE RANGE

Homestead

China Lake

Trona

Inyokern

Westend

Ridgecrest

Pinnacles National
Natural Landmark

Johannesburg

395

Suggested Route

20 MILES

© 2000 HUNTER PUBLISHING, INC

same names, like Lola Travis, a dance hall madam who brought her girls from Cerro Gordo to Darwin. Bartenders, gamblers, store clerks, newspapermen, and so many more types followed the money. Some came to get rich and get out. Some came to build homes and stay, only to find the town deserted around them when the mines dwindled and word of another strike filtered into town. It became a lifestyle: follow the excitement to the latest boom town, throw up a tent and start serving your wares, whether it was whiskey, sex, lawyering, hardware or newsprint; then, when the boom faded, when the mines began to close, rush on to the next bonanza.

Much of Darwin's population came from Cerro Gordo. Rich silver and lead deposits were found there in 1874. Beaudry himself came, and built the town's water supply. Darwin began to die in 1876, when the smelter shut down and yet another camp – Bodie – exploded on the scene.

Bodie

Bodie is north of the Mojave in the Great Basin Desert. While it is some distance from Ridgecrest, it is the best-preserved mining town in the West, and there is a good written record of the town and the events that made it famous. Once the home of 10,000 miners, gamblers, townspeople, and ruffians, Bodie today is a silent wood and brick monument to the American West.

Gold was first found here in 1859, but that initial discovery was just a flash in the pan. A Rainbow Chaser by the name of Waterman "Bill" Bodey panned the small stream that cuts through the hills north of Mono Lake. With three other wanderers, he struck a little gold; they followed the flakes upstream till the lay of the land told them they'd found the source. They posted claims and started digging.

Author Remi Nadeau gives another story of how the discovery occurred. He says that Bodey was out hunting for dinner, and he winged a rabbit that disappeared down its hole. Bodey began digging after the wounded rabbit, and discovered several small gold nuggets.

However he made his strike, Bill Bodey wasn't a hero or even a very reputable character. He had abandoned everything to chase the rainbow of gold and silver in the far West. He also was a person that most people stood upwind from. About 5 feet 7 inches tall, he was described by one contemporary as the dirtiest person he'd ever met. Reportedly, he was from Poughkeepsie, New York, where he'd been a tinsmith before walking out on a wife and six children to go prospecting. He was in on the excitement in Virginia City, but missed out on striking it rich or even finding any paydirt in the Nevada gold and silver fields. His strike would not make him rich, for he died not long after. The mining district and rowdy city that grew out of it was named for him, even if the spelling was rather casual.

The original strike was made in 1859. There wasn't much to it, however; no one got rich and the town faded to a few miners and stores. But in 1876, the small town's fortunes changed. A cave-in at the Bunker Hill mine (later renamed the Standard) exposed a rich body of gold ore. A boom began that built a city overnight.

When word of the vein reached nearby camps, once again the excitement was on. Bodie became the newest boomtown, and just about the last big strike of the gold rush era. By February, 1878, the town was overrun with prospectors and camp followers who endured the wind and snow while living in a tent city for the chance at getting their share of Bodie gold. By the end of 1878 over 600 buildings stood where just two years before there were only a few ramshackle cabins. Over 3,000 hookers, cardsharps, clerks, and miners roamed the hills where Bill Bodey had prospected some 20 years before.

The real town, and the legend, of Bodie was born. It was the wild and woolly West, a place where men worked, played, and died with their boots on, with few of the comforts of home.

Fortunes came out of the hills, and fortunes were passed across the tables at the Bonanza, Champion, Rifle Club, and 20 other saloons on the main street. At its peak, Bodie boasted of two banks, one of the biggest red light districts in the West, four daily newspapers, three breweries, and at least six hotels. From the first, gunplay and claim jumping were regular occurrences.

Grant Smith came to Bodie in 1879, at the tender age of 14. He worked as a telegraph messenger boy, and years later, published an account of his years in Bodie. He said: "Bodie was unique; it was the last of the old time mining camps; the last of the pioneer days in California. The leading spirits of the town were 'mining camp men' from California and Nevada. These were eager, young adventurers from the ends of the earth."

Smith's "mining camp men" were the ones who came after the prospectors and built a town around their find. They were doctors, lawyers, gamblers, bartenders, merchants, and camp followers.

"These men were virile, enthusiastic, and free living; bound by few rules of conventional society, though with an admirable code of their own: liberal minded, generous to a fault, square dealing, and devoid of pretense and hypocrisy. Besides the business and professional men, there were hundreds of saloonkeepers, hundreds of gamblers, hundreds of prostitutes, many Chinese, and an unusual number of what we called Bad Men. 'The Bad Man From Bodie' was a current phrase of the time throughout the West. In its day, Bodie was more widely known for its lawlessness than for its riches."

Bodie was a magnet for all kinds of people during its short shining days. Gold and silver were plentiful; jobs were readily available and paid exceptionally well. But Bodie, at least in its early days, was lacking in comforts outside of the bars and the red light district.

According to Smith's account, "All of the conditions in Bodie tended to make men reckless." They were in a remote, barren, sparsely settled country – "a land that God forgot" – practically without government and law. "It was a refuge for the lawless, with almost no conveniences of living." The town had "poor housing, limited water supply, no sanitary regulations, a harsh climate, forbidding surroundings, [there were no] warm cheerful places to go except the saloons [and the] red light district."

At this time in Bodie's history there were no hospitals, no churches, and no theaters; many people lived in tents in the surrounding hills. But that didn't last long. With the wealth pouring out of the ground, hundreds of people came to join the excitement. In his *Guide to Bodie and Eastern Sierra Historic Sites*, George Williams III describes a war of words between a Truckee newspaper and a Bodie newspaper. The Truckee paper printed a prayer from a little girl

Mojave Desert

whose family was moving to Bodie: "Goodbye, God! We are going to Bodie." The Bodie paper said the Truckee paper got it wrong; the prayer was actually "Good, by God! We are going to Bodie."

Dozens of bars sprang up, hundreds of prostitutes came to town, and dozens of gambling halls featuring faro and dice games opened seemingly overnight. Bodie was a place where a man could be relieved of his wages just by walking down the street and weakening to the enticements of the camp followers. Stagecoaches brought fresh grist for the Bodie mill, and stages left loaded with bullion, guarded by stern-faced gunmen. Crowds of hard men roamed the streets, a lusty crowd, boisterous with the hard-charging ways of life on the edge.

While it was a rowdy town, most of Bodie knew its place; the rowdiness generally was confined to the rough element in the red light district. As the town grew up, a few brave families came; but the families of Bodie were seldom bothered by the gunfights – of which an average of one a day occurred. The number of men killed in Bodie gunfights is estimated at several hundred. Even though violence was common, there were no bank or store robberies, no burglaries, and little petty theft, according to Smith. Even the violence was restricted to the red light district and the saloons; if one stayed away from these danger spots, Bodie was a reasonably safe place.

Smith claims that "One of the remarkable things about Bodie... was the respect shown by even the worst characters to the decent women and the children. Some of the best families in town lived [next to the] red light district, and the women and children could not move out of their houses without passing saloons and all sorts of terrible places. Yet I do not recall ever hearing of a respectable woman or young girl being in any manner insulted or even accosted by the hundreds of dissolute characters that were everywhere. In part, this was due to the respect that depravity pays to decency; in part to the knowledge that sudden death would follow any other course."

According to Smith, "one learned more about human nature in a few years than could be acquired in a city in a lifetime. There one saw the human animal in the raw. Yet, taking them for all in all, their virtues outweighed their vices. Their sins were mostly against themselves; their better natures showed in their attitude toward others. Somehow, all of the people – even those without the pale of mining camp respectability – showed some admirable traits. Ordinary men became transformed in that atmosphere."

Bodie's best days were short – from 1879 to 1882. The boom ended, but still some mining could be done; the population of the town fell to about 2,000 and hovered around 700 to 1000 in the 1890s. Bodie didn't die till 1914 when all mining stopped for the duration of World War I. There has been some mining in the area since, but no major strikes have been found.

The state park service took over the town in 1962. Rangers and volunteers have maintained and rebuilt about 5% of the structures that once stood in Bodie. A museum in the old miner's union hall is now open and several displays have been built, utilizing only the furnishings of the time.

Now, where fortunes were made and lost, where men died in gunfights and lived by the cut of the deck, the wind whispers and sighs through the deserted buildings. It's easy to imagine the ghosts of Bill Bodey and his fellow Rainbow Chasers and camp followers watching tourists wander their town, cameras strung around their necks instead of six-guns on their hips. Bodie stands as a testimony to them all — bad men and builders, miners and players, Rainbow Chasers and Desert Dancers – who lived the legends of the West.

Mojave Desert

If You Go

Wild Horse and Burro Corrals: *The corrals are just east of Ridgecrest near the Trona Road (Highway 178). They are open to the public for tours. The corrals can hold 1,300 animals, with the peak season running from fall through early spring. Business hours are Monday through Friday, 7:30 am to 4 pm, and it is closed for all federal holidays. Adoptions are arranged by appointment only; call ☎ (760) 446-6064. For further information about the Wild Horse and Burro Program contact David Sjaastad, California Desert District Wild Horse and Burro Program leader, ☎ (760) 384-5400. For additional information ☎ (800) 951-8720.*

Cerro Gordo: *This old mining town is located up a canyon, near Cerro Gordo peak, on the west side of Owen's Lake. The access is off State Route 136 near Keeler, which is southwest of Lone Pine.*

Darwin: *Darwin is south of State Route 190, between Olancha and Panamint Springs, west of Death Valley.*

Bodie: *This wonderful old ghost town is now a state park,* ☎ *(760) 647-6445. It is open only during the summer months, so call ahead for information. It is located well beyond Bishop, north of Mono Lake, about 175 miles north of Ridgecrest.*

Trona Pinnacles: *These Tufa formations are very unusual, and would be recognizable to Star Trek and other science fiction movie fans as they've been used as a location for other-worldly looks in many films. They are east of Ridgecrest and south of Trona, on the road to the Panamint Valley.*

Trona Pinnacles

The Land of Dreams

Off Highway 58, west of the town of Mojave, there's a place we like to stop when we have to leave the desert. From the bajada of Barren Ridge we can park and look over the western reaches of the desert, a view of a hundred miles or more. It's a very pleasant way to end the trip with a last stop on a trail that we've come to think of as ours. It wanders from the highway up to an abandoned mine back in the hills.

This is a busy part of the desert and there is a lot to watch when we make these stops. Not too far away is a huge civilian flight test center. To the north, the Rand and El Paso Mountains rise magnificently off the desert floor. To the south is the Palmdale/Lancaster/Quartz Hill complex, now a major metropolis backed by majestic mountains. At the bottom of the hill a long freight train labors up Tehachapi westward to the loop.

This view is the best and the worst of the desert, a view filled with emotionally charged contradictions.

At the Flight Test Center at the Mojave Airport, and farther on at Air Force Plant 42 in Lancaster/Palmdale, and the Edwards Air Force base in between, the desert is a field of dreams. From these locales man has reached higher and faster than any Rainbow Seeker would believe. Here are where the fastest planes come from, the newest technological wonders in stealth, and craft that can reach for the stars. The Space Shuttle was born here. New generations of warbirds, aerial people-haulers, cargo planes, and space vehicles are being developed on these fields. We see these strange birds in the sky here, nearly any day of the year.

In my eyes, this area is overdeveloped; too many people, huge tracts of homes, too many new industrial buildings, and too many paved roads replacing fine old trails. I suspect local developers would disagree. Cheap land and proximity to Los Angeles is a dangerous combination. It seems that each time we visit, hundreds of new homes have sprouted out of the desert sand. A new rail line carries commuters to their work in the city quickly and efficiently, supplementing a very nice freeway to the San Fernando Valley. I can't blame the newcomers; if I had to work in Los Angeles, here is where I would live.

Driving through **Palmdale** or **Lancaster** is a study in contradictions. A new Lexus sedan will be stopped at the red light next to a 30-year-old pickup truck. A ragtop flat-fender Jeep, built during the big war, will be in the lane next to a Dodge minivan. New housing

Mojave Desert

developments look as if they are transplanted from Los Angeles, with houses crowded together wearing same-looking red tile roofs set in tiny, green yards and designed with floor plans that repeat every third house. But down the street are some old desert ranches that sprawl around a large sandy lot filled with huge shade trees and tired old cars. And nearby, along some of the trails, you see the signs of people who do not respect the desert. Their discarded tires, old mattresses, and trash piles are obscene. For all that, we have a contradictory love for the Antelope Valley.

Some really fine people live here. On our trips to the Mojave we often start with a night at the **Essex House**, in Lancaster, where we are treated like family. The bartender gives us hugs when we walk in. The maid brings us extra coffee kits, knowing one pot is never enough for us. On the rare occasions when I'm by myself, the manager will wait for Suz's nightly call, then give her hell for not being there. It's an attitude you'll find all over the desert, once you take the time and make the effort to know the people; they care, and don't mind showing it.

The Essex House has a place in aviation history as well. They've serviced the fliers and technicians who built and operate these mechanical wonders for decades. On the walls of the lobby are dozens of signed photos of aircraft, presented to the hotel in appreciation for their legendary hospitality. In the hotel bar, stickers from flight groups, air forces, test groups, associations, and companies around the world decorate the walls and panels. The talk at the bar and the lobby is always air-related, and the collection of accents heard range from deep South, Western drawl, hard Yankee, English, Australian, and a few dozen other worlds far away from these desert lands.

Here in this valley you can see the best and the worst examples of interaction with the desert. While some people tear down, others build up. Not far from Rosamond – between Lancaster and Mojave – is the **Exotic Feline Breeding Compound**, a place that is working to restore endangered species of cats around the world. Several state parks are in this area; as the area grows, people feel the need to preserve the past and the land. Also, good people are making good efforts to clean up the mess other people leave on the desert.

Awareness of the delicate nature of the desert environment is growing and there is much less abuse. For those who won't "tread lightly" there are laws now to make them. These laws are needed most this close to civilization. As Dennis Casebeir said, "We don't close the freeway because someone speeds."

Another issue in this strange land: a huge mountain north of Rosamond is disappearing. Large, open pit mining operations create their own ecology. For an immense area, the land is totally given over to the mine's needs; vegetation and animal life is moved out or killed, and after the ore is processed, the tailings destroy even more land. New badlands are born. Little can grow in this wasteland, not until nature revitalizes the soil in its own way.

It is easy to accept an open pit mine that has been around for a while. It is land being used for the purpose of human growth and development, like a shopping mall or a housing development. It is a fact of life, a part of the scenery, not necessarily good or evil, just present.

Watching an open pit come into existence is another thing.

North of Rosamond the Golden Queen Mining Company, a Canadian corporation, is tearing down **Soledad Mountain**. The mountain is dying, as are the plants and animals that once thrived there. Valuable minerals will come out of that mountain and find their way into our lives, and the mountain will be gone.

It's all being done properly; the company filed its environmental impact reports, got all its myriad permits and licenses from the state and federal governments, and will undoubtedly restore the land to some semblance of what it was before. And most likely, in hundreds of years, the creosote and Joshua will come back to shelter the rattlesnakes and jackrabbits, as well as a desert tortoise or two.

The mountain has been mined for more than 100 years. Underground chasms criss-cross beneath the desert sand, where gold and silver veins were chased in the old-fashioned way with tunnels. But it is more efficient now to rip open the earth and chemically remove the product, so the mountain is dying. Every time we pass it we see more of Soledad Mountain is gone. I try to memorize how it looks, and try to imagine how it will look when it is completely gone.

Mojave Desert

There is a lot to do in the Palmdale/Lancaster/Quartz Hill area. Check the state parks section of the *Appendix* and you'll see that most of the state's desert parks are within a few miles of these cities. At **Air Force Plant 42** in Palmdale, two big, beautiful SR-71's – the highest-flying, fastest plane ever built – are on display. At **Edwards Air Force Base** there's a visitor center and a museum that is well worth your time. And always watch the sky when you're within a hundred miles of Mojave; strange things often fly around here.

If You Go

Palmdale is the first desert city you encounter coming north from Los Angeles on Highway 14. Lancaster is a little farther. Air Force Plant 42 is between the two towns on the Sierra Highway – and you won't miss the huge buildings in the complex, nor the SR-71s parked on the north side of the plant (near Lockheed's main gate).

The *Exotic Feline Breeding Compound*, ☎ (661) 256-3331, is east of Rosamond. Traveling on Highway 14 from Palmdale, go north to Rosamond; take the Rosamond Boulevard exit, turn left (west), drive about four miles to the Mojave-Tropico Road, where you'll turn right (north); then follow the signs to the compound.

Farther west on Rosamond Boulevard is the **Willow Springs International Raceway**, ☎ (661) 256-2471, where cars and motorcycles are tested almost daily, and racing goes on almost every weekend.

On *Edwards Air Force Base* is the Dryden Flight Research Center, home of the Space Shuttle and many other exotic aircraft. The visitor center and gift shop is open 7:45 am to 3:45 pm during the week. Tours of Dryden Center for individuals or groups can be arranged during the week, but are by reservation only. ☎ (661) 258-3446 or 3460 to arrange the tour. The entrance to the base is about 15 miles east of the town of Mojave on Highway 58.

Tell the folks at the Essex House hello for us.

Barstow & the Central Mojave

Rainbow Basin

We were standing on a ledge at Rainbow Basin. Dally – a cow dog, a great little Australian shepherd who has been desert dancing with Suz and me for the last couple of trips – lifted her nose and sniffed the trail of a burro that passed here just moments before. She's unsure of the odor; Dally knows horses and cattle well, and has met the occasional burro before, but the smell of a burro in the wild is something indefinably new.

Rock formations at Rainbow Basin.

Rainbow Basin. It's one of those rare places in the world that lives up to its name and exceeds its advance billing. Not many desert tourist books mention this place, or give it more than a paragraph or two.

It is located north of Barstow and west of the Fort Irwin Road. I could spend a lifetime here.

It doesn't look like a canyon or even a basin, but it's been called both. Rainbow Basin is a natural cut in the side of a mountain that exposes the eons in splashes of color and layered waves, all cast in stone. It is a mishmash of shapes, colors and surreal formations, yet there is logic here; it is the logic of water and wind, and gravity, and the movement of the earth over incomprehensible periods of time. I don't understand it, but it's some comfort to know that someone else does.

Dally – she could care less about the logic of the geology around us – loves the desert. She is arthritic, and the young pup that chased cows for a living is no longer. She now lives in the Central Valley where the damp winters give her hell. That's why she started coming on these trips and, from the first, she has loved the dry air, the strange smells of creosote and the feel of sand underfoot. She hits the trails running, driven to know this strange land, and she is comfortable in it, as happy as any time since her cowboy-owner, a young man named Dennis Walker, left her with Suz when he moved to Oklahoma. Perhaps the freedom of the open spaces calls to her spirit as it does to mine.

Now, in Rainbow Basin, Dally has found another path to explore. We hiked up a narrow arroyo, following the fresh tracks of the burro, and found what could be common opal; Dally has an eye for such stuff. The plant life was minimal: a little grass, a lonely creosote, and a small Joshua. Odd, to see one creosote bush; they live in colonies, and there should have been more, but perhaps they were washed away in the El Niño floods last spring. On the top of the canyon walls, on the hills forming the sides of the basin, many Joshuas, stand guard over the mountain like warrior sentinels poised to strike anyone who debases this lovely place.

Lovely, but strange. Science fiction movies should be, and probably are, filmed here. This place is other-worldly, a land that can't possibly exist on the same planet that holds forests and lakes and lush meadows. None of these things seem possible when you're looking at Rainbow Basin.

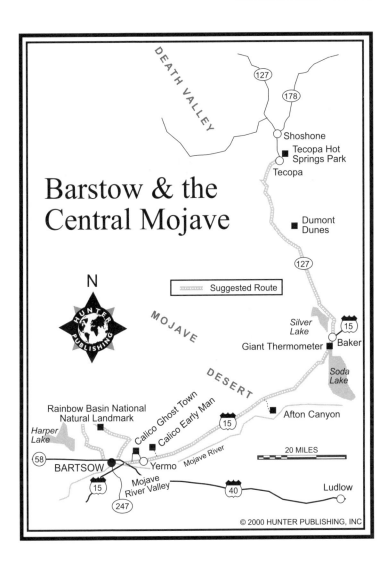

Barstow & the
Central Mojave

Mojave Desert

The Bureau of Land Management has built a road through here, a dirt track that winds through narrow gorges and gouges. With each turn something new, something stunningly simple or incomprehensibly complex hangs over the roadway, each more colorful and fascinating than the previous. According to the experts, this was once a lush marsh and the home of many prehistoric creatures. Miocene horses, camels, mastodons, saber-toothed cats and a million insects once lived here. While many of the fossil remains have been excavated, many have not and are visible in the rock.

This is a beautiful geologic wonderland, with nearly every color of the rainbow represented. There are fault lines, plunge pools, mud caves, hogbacks, and other rock formations that defy being named or described. Some of the fossils found in Rainbow Basin are now on display in museums around the country. These animals are now extinct, but many of their ancestors now live in Africa. So many have been discovered here that geologists call the period when they roamed the North American continent the Barstovian Stage.

Rainbow Basin.

Barstow

We came here from Barstow, the crossroads of the desert, this morning. We had taken the long way, of course, following a four-wheel-drive trail that took us miles and hours out of our way. It had been one of those lazy, Sunday-drive kind of trips; slow and easy, taking time to explore, wandering over new roads, just more or less following the compass and the map in the general direction of Rainbow Basin. I got lost for a while, but it didn't matter; I knew the way out. Besides, it was a day for adventuring, with crystal blue skies and winter-cool weather. All I had to do was stay off Fort Irwin, a military reservation with a huge playground for tank drivers and other ground warriors. However, if I had known what Rainbow Basin was really like I wouldn't have wasted the time wandering around. I would have driven here directly on the easy road. Barstow is only about 10 miles southeast of Rainbow Basin.

Barstow is famous as a waystop between Los Angeles and Las Vegas. It would be hard to avoid making a rest stop here on the way to Gambler's Heaven; the hours of freeway travel demand it. As a result, Barstow is home to the world's busiest McDonald's, as well as numerous truck stops and motels. It's a railroad town, too, with a huge Southern Pacific switchyard and tracks that lead to the transportation centers on the coast and in the Midwest. In the early years it was a major supply point for desert mining interests.

This is a typical desert town, in that the desert overrides man's ambition to turn every community into a carbon copy of other cities. Sand and creosote forms the normal landscaping here; eastern trees and bushes do not do well. The older houses and buildings are mostly made of adobe, which is just a fancy word for a type of mud that makes a great building material for the desert – the mud bricks provide excellent insulation from the heat. Houses and yards, normally hidden by shade trees, are exposed to the full brunt of the sun; colors fade to white and wood turns permanently gray. Things that are thrown away in every town are also thrown away here – but they do not quickly rot in the desert, or get covered up by native grasses and bushes. A McDonald's wrapper from years ago might still be visible, half-covered by blow sand but still an eyesore. Old cars degenerate into junky hulks, then remain in a state of suspended animation, parked in someone's yard for all to see. So, to someone who is used to oak-lined streets and the camouflage of nature, desert towns are downright ugly and poor-looking. Barstow, at least along Highway 58 and on the outskirts, is no exception. But if you take a little time to look beneath the surface, it's a pretty fine place. Just don't expect this or any desert town to meet your expectations of a city back east, or on the coast.

Desert people know Barstow as the central city of the Mojave. There are numerous motels with reasonable prices, desert information cen-

Mojave Desert

ters, and the **Museum of the Mojave River Valley**. Nearby is **Calico Ghost Town**, a great place for kids of all ages; it's a mining town that was restored as a tourist attraction by the Knott's Berry Farm people. Near Calico is the **Calico Early Man Site**. Primitive tools and artifacts, which some estimate to be as much as 200,000 years old, have been found on the shores of Lake Manix. This site is open for guided tours Wednesday through Sunday.

Ufologists love this area. At least one tourist trap along the freeway to Las Vegas specializes in all sorts of UFO stuff from books to t-shirts and much more. The owners are not little green men and women, however. They appear to be as human as any other Californian.

The best thing about Barstow, in my mind, is that it's an hour away from the Mojave National Preserve, and deep in the heart of the Mojave. From Barstow it isn't far to some truly wonderful places: The Mojave Trail; Rainbow Basin; Tecopa; Afton Canyon.

These names sing to me when I read them on a map or a highway sign. They seem to belong in a simpler, wilder time, where the choices are clear, where life is a matter of survival first, everything else second.

From Barstow, exploring any of these places is within a day's drive. Heading northeast on Interstate 15, you'll pass Calico then the exit for **Afton Canyon**, often called the Grand Canyon of the Mojave. That's a bit pretentious, and Afton is spectacular in its own right. It doesn't need to be compared to the big ditch. There's a popular BLM campground and an off-road vehicle play area.

The **Mojave River** formed the canyon. The Mojave is only a small stream here normally, and to the east it fades away altogether. But in Afton Canyon, the river supports willows, tamarisks, and a rich growth of smaller plants; it is an oasis that has been popular with travelers for hundreds and hundreds of years. The walls of the canyon expose the volcanic collision of magma and sedimentary rock that formed these mountains, and are a playground of color and fascinating vistas.

Farther along the freeway is another famous desert town: **Baker**, with its population of only 500 intrepid desert dwellers. Here you'll find a world-famous thermometer with electric-light numbers that often are in the three-digit range. The thermometer is billed as the world's tallest. It measures 134 feet tall, one foot for every degree of the hottest day recorded in Death valley. Next to the base of the thermometer is a desert information center with a bookstore. It's operated by the US Park Service and offers details about Death Valley and the Mojave National Preserve.

Baker is the northern entrance to the Preserve, but is probably better known as the southern entrance to Death Valley. Northward out of Baker a two-lane (paved) highway follows Salt Creek to the Amargosa River, then on to the towns of Shoshone and Tecopa, and into Death Valley National Park.

It's a beautiful drive, for a paved road. **Silurian Lake**, a typical Mojave playa, parallels the road. The Silurian Hills east of the lake bed beckon and, in winter, a far-off peak shines with snow, a startling contrast to the baked-dry brown of the playa. Farther on, the **Salt Hills** stand next to the **Dumont Dunes**. The Salt Hills are a colorful mix of rock and the dunes are creamy tan soft sand sculptures that are as much as 400 feet high. The **Little Dumont Dunes** are next to the road; the big monsters are several miles off the highway, but clearly visible.

A few miles north, the highway intersects with the **Old Spanish Trail**. This route was popular with horse thieves in the early 1800s. They'd ride from Santa Fe, New Mexico, to the Spanish missions on the coast, to steal horses and cattle. Bringing them back along the Spanish Trail was a wild ride to **Tecopa**, where the pursuing posse would usually give up the chase.

These communities are mostly ghost towns in summer, when Baker's thermometer hits 120 or more. But in winter, especially during November's '49er Days, Shoshone and Tecopa become trailer cities. Motor homes of all descriptions, from 40-year-old clunkers to new, sleek mansions on wheels, descend upon this area, piloted mostly by snowbirds from the northeast. The snowbirds especially like Tecopa, where hot springs are the big draw.

Tecopa is on the edge of a marshy lake, fed by natural springs in a land where it almost never rains. The ground water, even from wells

Mojave Desert

400 feet deep, comes out of the ground at 120°. The hot springs have been a retreat for arthritis sufferers for several generations.

Not far beyond Tecopa and Shoshone is Death Valley National Park. We'll get there, but first it's time to head down to the largest and most empty part of this desert: the Mojave National Preserve.

Talc transfer station near Tecopa.

If You Go

Rainbow Basin: *Well worth the trip. In Barstow, take Old Highway 58 to Irwin Road; go north on Irwin Road; turn west (left) on Fossil Bed Road. Follow the signs to Rainbow Basin.*

Calico Ghost Town *and* **Calico Early Man Site:** *These tourist attractions are about eight miles east of Barstow on Interstate 15.*

Afton Canyon: *The Afton exit is about 37 miles east of Barstow on Interstate 15. A graded, well-maintained dirt road leads to a BLM campground (no telephone) in the canyon.*

Baker: *Baker is 60 miles east of Barstow on Interstate 15. All services are available.*

Tecopa Hot Springs: *Head north from Baker on State Road 127. Turn right at the Old Spanish Trail Road (about 60 miles north of Baker). At the general store in Tecopa, stop for a while and talk to the local characters and visiting snowbirds – it's a relaxing visit where you'll meet lots of friendly people. Then turn left on Tecopa Hot Springs Road. The springs are two miles ahead. Anybody who doesn't really like heat should consider this trip a winter-only excursion.*

The Mojave National Preserve

The Mojave National Preserve defies comprehension. It is a lonely triangle of land, bordered by major freeways north and south and the Colorado River to the east. By their sheer weight, the numbers describing the land become meaningless: 1.4 million acres, 16 mountain ranges, 10,000 mining claims yet only four active mines. Geologically, it is fascinating: coal-black lava flows, shimmering salt lake beds, purple mountain ranges, layer upon layer of rocks – some that are as old as a billion years and others less than a thousand.

To the first Americans who traveled through this area by foot, horse and wagon, this uncommonly beautiful country was a peculiar form of hell. Dry and desolate, it was and still is. Especially to those men and women coming from the lush forests of the east and south, the desert was a barren expanse to be barely tolerated before arriving in the Promised Land of California.

The first time I saw this empty triangle of land, I saw a place I wanted to know. It is a place I could live in forever. To call it vast and scenic is to call the sky blue. It's a fact, but just as the blue of the sky can

Mojave Desert

have many hues, the vastness of the eastern Mojave is more than a vague description of its size. The vastness is a palpable force, an assault on the senses.

You stand on a rock and look forever. You're a mile high, standing among piñon and scrub pine, looking down into white and brown playas and the blue mountain ranges that rise from them. The startlingly black lava flows are so dark they soak up the sun and throw back no colors, no reflections. It is a black so strong you think a cloud is blocking the sun, but not a single cloud is in the sky. When you're in the Joshua forests they stretch to the horizon, a crazy jangle reaching to the heavens. Jagged rock peaks jut out of the ground – but just a few miles away sand dunes climb to the sky. These soft hills are a startling contrast to the granite pinnacles.

It's incredibly valuable land to you and me, and to the few cattlemen and miners that live here – a photographer's heaven (a lifetime of shooting would not capture it all). But to others, it's worthless. The eastern Mojave is one of the few areas of California that did not explode with people in the first 150 years of the state's history. In the early 1900s there was a flurry of activity, with railroads, mining and cattle ventures, and the brave souls that farmed the dry land in Lanfair Valley. But few of these efforts lasted much longer than a desert storm. Except for a few continuing operations, mining died away and agriculture did not take off except for far-flung cattle operations. So there was little reason for anyone to be out here and throughout most of the 20th century; the area remained the domain of a few ranchers, desert rats, and miners.

When the Mojave National Preserve was formed in 1994, it put the land in a curious state of limbo. It was a controversial act that placed the desert under the firm control of environmentalists. The National Park Service administers the land and all activities must now conform to their goals and methods, which are not yet clearly defined; there is no management plan written for the area that clearly states the agency's goals and methods. Trails and roads to petroglyphs, magnificent scenery, and many treasures have been gated and locked; we, the people who own those treasures, can't get to them. Environmentalists would say of course we can see them – we just have to get out of our cars and hike. But the reality is that not many people are in good enough physical condition to walk a dozen miles with cameras and survival gear in 110° heat. We can't prospect for gold or pick up rocks. However, because all growth and development is stopped, the Preserve also creates a link to our history and to the natural desert environment that will survive the changing times and be passed on to future generations. It's a vexing issue.

Not all land uses were stopped with the creation of the Preserve. Cattle and sheep ranching as well as some mining still go on. At the present time about 1,200 miles of road remain open. While some of these are paved two-lane roads and others are well-maintained dirt roads, most are rough four-wheel-drive routes.

A few paved roads cross the Preserve from north to south. **Kelbaker Road** takes off from Baker on Interstate 15, heads southeasterly to Kelso, then passes the dunes on through Granite Pass to meet Interstate 40. The **Cima Road** exits 15 about 40 miles east of Baker, passes through the settlement of **Cima** (home of the only store in the Preserve; ring the bell outside the front door for service) and proceeds to Kelso and the Kelbaker Road. The **Morning Star Mine Road** will take a traveler from Cima to the main highway to Searchlight. Another stretch of pavement exits Interstate 40 to bring tourists to the Providence Mountains and the Mitchell Caverns. Farther east, the **Goffs-Lanfair-Ivanpah Road** is one of the main north-south routes in the Preserve and is partially paved. It provides the easternmost link between I-40 on the south and I-15 on the north.

Numerous dirt roads take off from these paved highways. Some of them are graded and well-maintained. Most, however, are my kind of roads: dirt tracks, following the contours of the land, empty of fences and signs.

But even if a traveler chooses to stay on the pavement, the Preserve is a panoply of desert vistas; your fingers will itch for a camera. Southeast of Baker, east of the Kelbaker Road, are numerous cinder cones and lava flows. Some of the flows in the area of the Preserve are from eruptions that occurred just 1,000 to 6,000 years ago, an eyeblink in geological time. Some geologists say this area could still be active.

Mojave Desert

Along the Cima Road.

Along the Cima Road is an unusual hill: the **Cima Dome**. It's a 10-mile-wide inverted gold pan, covered with a Joshua forest and, on its eastern slope, the remains of an ancient volcano, now known as Teutonia Peak. Scientists say the Dome is the remnant of a magma batholith.

Southward is the town of **Kelso**, with its famous depot. Not much of the town remains. Founded in 1906, it was once an active railroad and mining town.

South and west of Kelso are some of the most magnificent sand dunes in the Western Hemisphere. The **Kelso Dunes** are "booming" dunes, where the sound of the sand carried by the wind makes a variety of noises. The dunes themselves are immense: 45 square miles of sand; some of the dunes are 600 feet high. They are formed by sands that are picked up by the wind in the Mojave River sink and the sandy Devil's Playground, then deposited on the windward side of the Providence Mountains.

To the east of the dunes, and across the Providence Mountains, the **Mitchell Caverns** are an intriguing underground vista. They are cool: a constant 65°. The caverns are limestone and were used as shelters by the Chemehuevis Indians. There are archaeological artifacts as well as colorful stalagmites and stalactites. Now a state park, the caverns were first developed as an attraction by Jack Mitchell, a prospector, during the 1930s. Now state rangers lead 90-minute excursions through the caverns and narrow passageways between September 16 and June 15.

All these places, and these roads, are worth seeing; but perhaps the best treasure on the Preserve is a pair of tracks that cross the middle of it. This famous trail is the **Mojave Road**, one of the early wagon routes that brought American pioneers to California. This trail is unique in that for most of this 138-mile stretch it is in much the same condition as the pioneers would have found it, and a lot of the trail passes through country that is virtually unchanged since prehistoric times. The road bisects the Mojave National Preserve, wandering from waterhole to waterhole, and is mostly a four-wheel-drive trail. So of course I have to drive it. You can ride along with me, next chapter.

Mojave Desert

Exploring the Mojave Road.

Dennis Casebier

This trail would have faded from sight except for the curiosity and perseverance of one man: Dennis Casebier.

We caught up with Dennis at his home in Goffs, on the south side of the Mojave National Preserve. He moved to this 113-acre desert ranch when he retired in 1990. With his wife, Jo Ann, and innumerable friends, he has built a natural and historical center that is a gold mine of displays, photographs, and reference materials in a library of more than 6,000 books.

Stamp mill at Goffs.

He came to the desert in 1954 as a young Marine stationed at Twentynine Palms. Born in Kansas in 1934, he found the desert a new and different world. It called his name, however, and most weekend passes were spent camping and hiking in what is now Joshua Tree National Park. Out of these weekends came a love for the desert lands that kept this Kansas native on the desert for most of his adult life.

After his time in the Marines, Dennis Casebier (pronounced case-beer) returned to Kansas and went to college. He could hardly wait to return to the California desert, and upon graduating he took a job as a Navy missile scientist at Corona in 1960. His passion for the desert grew, and his training as a scientist blended well with his other passions: curiosity, truth, and history. The result is a body of work that will be a resource for generations to come.

When he returned to his desert in 1960 he found it had changed. Joshua Tree had become too busy for him and, like a true Rainbow Chaser, his eyes were drawn to the far horizon, where blue mountains and dry canyons beckoned. He methodically surveyed the high Mojave and the southern low Colorado/Sonoran desert. He bought a full set of USGS 15-minute quadrangle maps, from the Owens Valley to the Mexican border, and studied them.

"The eastern Mojave drew me," he said. "It was similar in elevation to Joshua Tree, but not as populated, and it interested me. Then I kept seeing references to 'Old Government Road' on the maps. This excited my curiosity and I wanted to know more about it."

His quest for knowledge took him from the high desert to the National Archives in Washington. He rediscoverd the exciting story of a 150-year-old wagon trail that had been almost forgotten: The Mojave Road.

During his career as a scientist for the Navy, he made many trips to Washington, so many that eventually he rented an apartment there. He spent his evenings at the National Archives finding any record he could that related to the Mojave Road. He microfilmed the records and brought them home. Back on the Mojave, he followed the trail and found it still in existence, even in use as a road in some areas. He identified the sites of five Army outposts as well as other settlements along the way. Over the years he assembled a full record of the last 150 years along the Road.

"I can tell you the names of every soldier that was stationed on the Road, and when he was here," he said. "I can even tell you the color of his eyes."

By 1980 he had accumulated a tremendous amount of information about the Mojave Road, and interest in his project was growing. The Bureau of Land Management wanted to mark the trail for public access, so others could share the experience of traveling the road. But Dennis was concerned that the impact of many more travelers would destroy the road – or worse, environmentalist pressure would encourage the BLM to close it off forever.

"This isn't a pristine wagon trail. In fact, not a foot of the trail hasn't been driven by motorized vehicle," Casebier said. "We weren't the first to drive it. There were Model A parts along the trail."

As interest grew in his research he formed the **Friends of the Mojave Road** (no telephone). This group worked with the BLM to identify the route of the trail and to create a trail guide for others. While the BLM wanted to put up signs, the Friends insisted that no signs be allowed; the road would be navigated by following rock cairns located at strategic intervals.

"This did two things for the road," Casebier explains. "First, to travel the Road you have to buy the *Mojave Road Guide*. This gives us a chance to tell people how they should behave, and I believe if you tell people what they should do they'll do it. This has worked. If you drive the trail now, you won't see where people have driven off the trail or left trash behind. The second thing is, not having signs reduces the numbers of people who drive the Road.

"Each one of us has some impact when we drive the Road. At a certain point that does no harm, and even does some good in preserving the Road. But at some point the numbers increase to where they do harm. Fort Piute has been disappearing one rock at a time; the walls used to be much higher. No one goes out there to tear down the fort, but they may take one rock as a memento, a trophy of their visit. Enough people have done this that the walls are almost gone."

Casebier points out that the Road, while not a particularly tough four-wheel-drive trail, is a dangerous place.

"You can die out there," he said. "And the people who want to go see the trail need to be equipped properly. We once had a lady come here to Goffs who wanted to go to Fort Piute – alone in her Chevy. She just wouldn't believe what we told her, that she'd never make it in that car, and could die trying to walk out. You are alone and many, many miles from help when you're on that road."

Preserving the Road – keeping it alive for access by people who will respect the land, tread lightly, and preserve the heritage it represents – remains a critical interest of Dennis Casebier.

"The establishment of the Mojave National Preserve will eventually destroy the Mojave Road," he asserts.

The Preserve was created by the 1994 Desert Protection Act, and control of this land was transferred from the BLM to the National

Park Service. The philosophy of the BLM allows multiple use; thus, mining, cattle and sheep ranching, and recreation could co-exist on the same land.

"The Park Service's business is preservation. If the Road becomes more heavily used, at some point they won't let it happen any more; they will shut it down. If we lose the Mojave Road, we lose our Americana. It becomes a Disneyland like Grand Canyon, Yellowstone, and Yosemite."

Shutting down access to desert lands has become a problem for many desert people, including Casebier. The Wilderness Act created many new wilderness areas throughout the California deserts. Designating these lands as "Wilderness" means that vehicles can no longer travel the roads within the designated areas.

"So what happens when people can't go four-wheeling and exploring where they used to, and have to hike in to these places? They won't go," Casebier pointed out. "This pushes more and more people onto lands that are not protected and increases the environmental damage in those areas."

Casebier acknowledges that some people are destructive to the natural environment.

"However, when the speed limit is 65 on the freeway, most people will go that speed. You don't close the freeway because someone is traveling at 90. You throw him in jail and let the rest of us go on."

The depth of Casebier's concern, and the value of his opinions, are clear when you visit his 113-acre desert home. It is a lifetime accumulation of knowledge and work, with displays devoted to the desert tortoise, mining, the railroads, and old buildings. The capstone is the Goffs schoolhouse, which is fully restored. With a group he helped form – the **Mojave Desert Heritage and Cultural Association** – he is in the process of turning his collection into a museum and resource center.

It will be a fitting memorial to a man who dedicated his life to understanding the Mojave, and has revived the past and made it a living experience through the Mojave Road (see below for details on the Mojave Road).

Mojave Desert

The Desert Tortoise Capital of the World, Goffs.

Health Resort or Money Machine?

The former resort known as Zzyzx was a beehive of activity in the mid-20th century. Located near Soda Lake on the far western edge of the Preserve, Zzyzx was built by a radio preacher/healer/doctor who touted the medicinal powers of the mud from Soda Springs. The resort was a popular health spa until the Bureau of Land Management shut it down in the 1970s.

Zzyzx is not an Indian name. The doctor created it to be the last word in the English language. Curtis Howe Springer was an interesting case study among desert characters. It would be easy to characterize him as a fraud and a charlatan, as some did and do; but he did many kind and charitable works as well. You paid what you could afford to stay at his spa and take his cure. If you had nothing, it was free. He brought men from skid row in Los Angeles and put them to work at his spa. He also sold his teas and salts from Soda Springs as a curative for many ailments. The AMA called him the "King of Quacks." The IRS accused him of tax evasion. But others found him to be truly dedicated to bringing other people happiness through good health.

The BLM evicted him in 1974. He was operating his spa on land that was never "patented" – he had filed mining claims, but never got clear title on the spa and resort he had built. The BLM was able to reclaim the land for the US Government.

Curtis Howe Springer died in 1985. His spa was taken over by the California State University and turned into the California Desert Studies Consortium. While it is publicly owned, public access is rigidly regulated.

The Singing Sands of the Kelso Dunes

The song of the desert has many verses, and one of the most expressive is the music made by the wind. You'll hear it day or night, its tune changing with the land.

Some people say the sands at Kelso sing with their own unique song. Some claim that these dunes moan, roar, hum and buzz, make drumming noises or violin sounds in a concert orchestrated by the wind. They claim the sounds are modified by the temperature, the moisture in the air or in the dune, the speed or direction of the wind, the listener's location on the dune, and the size and shape of any nearby obstacles.

But not everyone has heard them. I never have, but I have not spent much time on the Kelso Dunes. Neither have people I know who have spent many days and many nights there, listening for their song. Even so, I am reluctant to let it go. I want them to sing.

Just the thought of singing sands brings the imagination to life. Legends of lost souls, sand-drowned cities, and ghostly musicians arise from singing sand. These legends exist, among American natives and Sahara Bedouins alike.

Mojave Desert

The Mojave National Preserve is huge and empty. Except for the store at Cima (which may or may not be open) there are no services of any kind. Take plenty of emergency rations and extra water, and fill up your gas tank. Bring plenty of film for your camera; you'll use a lot. Goffs, Nipton, and Baker are the nearest sources for supplies, on the edge of the Preserve.

Depending on the carrier, cell phones work in many areas of the Preserve. If you get in trouble, give it a try.

Maps, pamphlets, and books are available at the Desert Information Centers operated by the National Park Service at Baker, Barstow, and Needles. Write for information at: **Mojave National Preserve Desert Information Center**, *PO Box 241, Baker, CA 92309;* ☎ *(760) 733-4040.*

Hotels/motels are available in Baker, Barstow, Needles, Searchlight (Nevada), and Primm (Nevada, at the state line on Interstate 15).

The Mojave Road

Fingers of fog dawdle on the Sierra foothills when I cross over Tehachapi to go find the Mojave Road. It's winter, and the desert has cooled nicely. My trail partner stayed at home this time, unable to make the journey. With a little trepidation but also a sense of adventure, I'm breaking the first rule of desert travel and starting out on my journey alone. I am alone, but not unprepared; I expect my cell phone, GPS, good maps, my water and emergency supplies to see me through. My destination is a pair of lonely tracks that run from Barstow to the Colorado River.

The Mojave Road was a main wagon trail for just two decades, after the Civil War. It was no longer needed when the railways came; they created an easier route to the south complete with oases on the bitter-dry deserts. But while it was used, the Mojave Road was a route plagued by hostile Indians, a lack of water, long stretches of sand, and rough hill climbs. For caravans of travelers and a handful of soldiers, it was a proving ground that brought out the best and the worst of them.

To those who took the Mojave Road by foot, horse and wagon, and the few men stationed along the road to defend it, this uncommonly beautiful country was a peculiar form of hell. It was, and still is, dry and desolate.

In the great westward migration to California, the Mojave Road was not an important player. Most travelers went north across Donner Pass, or south through the Colorado Desert. The road was primarily a supply route used by soldiers and freighters. Its 140 miles of dusty tracks are pretty much the same today as they were then. Thanks to the efforts of Dennis Casebier and the Friends of the Mojave Road, these old ruts cover ground pretty much as they did when the wagons rolled over them in the 1860s.

This unique situation came about because, unlike nearly every other major travel route on the frontier, the Mojave Trail did not evolve into a 20th-century superhighway. Better routes were found between the few cities worth going to in the area.

Water is everything on the desert, and the locations of watering holes determined the route of the trail. Water was found at the end of each day's drive (about every 20 to 30 miles, depending upon the terrain) and it was water that had to be reliable and safe. These springs were favored ambush sites, so each location had to be defended by a United States Army that was hard pressed to do it. So the Army established outposts, military camps of sometimes just two or three men, who spent their tours of duty protecting gold-seekers and farmers heading for a better life in the golden valleys near the coast. The Army felt it had to be done; by controlling the water, they controlled the road.

It was lonely, hard duty, and some of them died doing it. A few deserted. Others became generals. It was a place that brought out the best and the worst in people, as the desert does today.

Like most trails and even today's superhighways, the road was first an Indian path, used as a trade route. The Mojave Indians, who lived along the Colorado River, would travel to the coast, following the path that guaranteed water.

Father Francisco Garces

The first European to use the Mojave Trail was probably Father Francisco Garces in 1776.

Garces was an interesting desert character. Unlike most Spaniards, who remained along the coast or in the settlements of New Mexico, Padre Garces spent much of his life with the Indians, even going native, to the consternation of his cronies. He wandered the Southwest deserts alone, without a military escort, going from village to village, exploring the land and spreading the word of God. A fellow Franciscan, Pedro Font, told the authorities of the time that Garces "appears to be but an Indian himself.

" He would sit with the Indians for hours, and "with great gusto," eat foods that Font thought were "nasty and dirty." Font concluded, "God has created him solely for the purpose of seeking out these unhappy, ignorant, and rustic people."

Unfortunately, Garces' lifestyle eventually caught up with him. He was killed during an Indian uprising near Yuma.

When the Americans began pushing westward, Jedediah Smith, Kit Carson, John Fremont, and other mountain men came this way to reach the pueblos on the coast. When gold was found in 1849, most of the 'Niners went the northern route, but thousands followed the southern route and took the Mojave Road.

The Camel Experiment

In the late 1850s, Edward Beale undertook an experiment for the military: using camels to cross the Southwest. His camel trek across New Mexico and Arizona to the Mojave Road proved their worth, but muleskinners and freighters didn't like their sour tempers and Beale learned that they wouldn't make the transition to camels easily. The camels could have worked out, as Beale was happy with the performance of the surly animals. But the camel's biggest proponent in Washington, who could have merged them into the army's quartermaster corps, became preoccupied with certain other matters in the early 1860s. That man was Jefferson Davis, President of the Confederacy, and supporting any of Davis' ideas in Washington was not politically correct in the 1860s. So the camel experiment failed.

As the population of California grew in the 1850s and 60s, the Mojave Trail became a main southern freight route across California to Arizona. The trail also developed as a mail route, and that was when the military forts were established to keep the lines of communication open. These strongholds began at Fort Mojave, located on the Colorado River near present day Bullhead City, and ranged to Camp Cady, just outside Barstow.

Fort Mojave

Fort Mojave was established to suppress the Mojave Indians, whose warriors had come to resent the intrusions of the Americans traveling through their lands. The Mojaves were agrarians, growing corn and other crops along the Colorado River, and they were traders, who traveled frequently to the coast. They were hostages to their farms, however, and with the establishment of an Army fort on their land their warrior days were over.

While Fort Mojave worked well to keep the Mojave Indians subdued, the Chemehuevis Indians were not tied to the land and kept the US Army well occupied along the trail. In the grand tradition of the

Mojave Desert

Southwestern US tribes, these were excellent guerrilla fighters that could raid and fade away into desert dust. They traveled in small bands and any livestock along the trail was fair game. While only a few travelers were killed, the Army was forced to deal with the threat by establishing a military presence in the area.

The need for these camps faded, with the subjugation of the Indian threat and the construction of railroads south and north of the Mojave Road. When the railroads were built travelers found it easier to follow their tracks, as the railroads had water stops every five miles or so. The camps along the Mojave Road were abandoned eventually by the military, but civilian station tenders opened some of them as stagecoach stops or primitive roadhouses. Today a few remains are left of this legendary time, and following the Mojave Road brings us back to this era.

Travels Along the Mojave Road

Traveling the Mojave Road isn't a picnic. It's a two- or three-day excursion, best made in convoy with other four-wheelers. The trip begins on the shore of the **Colorado River**, at an elevation of 500 feet; by mile 54.8 you'll be at the head of **Cedar Canyon** at an elevation of 5,167 feet. During the winter you could hit a snowstorm. In summer it could be 120°, or a summer thunderstorm could bring heavy rain, hail and lightning. Any time of the year, you're a long way from help and city comforts.

> The first step in traveling the Mojave Trail is to get a copy of Dennis Casebier's *Mojave Road Guide*. It's indispensable. Casebier spent decades traveling the trail, and has an insatiable appetite for history and geology. This book is the culmination of his research and effort to preserve the trail. Mile-by-mile, he guides us over the passes and through the valleys, 138.8 miles of four-wheeling over three days.

There are few signs, and none on the trail itself. Casebier and his group, the Friends of the Mojave Road, have erected rock cairns at most intersections to show the way. Casebier's book starts at the Colorado River and travels the 138 miles westward to **Camp Cady**.

To cover the entire trail is a three-day wilderness adventure during which you'll find no services, no stores, no motels, and perhaps not a single other person. But portions of the trail can be traveled in shorter excursions. There are areas to avoid, unless you're in it for the challenge; but frankly, crossing the sandy expanse where the Mojave River becomes a floodplain, or Soda Lake, doesn't appeal. I've been stuck in sand and am not anxious to repeat it.

However, Dennis Casebier calls the floodplain a beautiful place to visit. According to Casebier, it's best in the spring: "… stop your vehicle (on firm ground, of course), shut off the engine, and walk out onto the sand. Fill up your senses with the buzzing of the bees, the flitting of the hummingbirds, and the fragrant bouquet of the desert willows." With a description like that, I know I'll have to go there one of these days.

I drove through **Searchlight** at 7 o'clock in the morning on a winter day, on my way to the Mojave Road. I've always loved that name: Searchlight, Nevada. Is it a beacon on the desert? I've seen the name on freeway signs, and wanted to find out what the town was like.

Well, it's small, a mining town, with a motel or two and a casino or two; gas stations, general stores, and a mine in the heart of town, all set in rocky desert hills. The gas was expensive and the clerk was busy arguing with one of her regulars. I still don't know what the town is like, but at least I've been there now, and can see it in my mind's eye when I think of it.

The morning was clear and bright, but a little windy, when I found where the Mojave Road crosses Highway 95 about 24 miles south of Searchlight, a few miles after both roads enter California. A rock cairn was on the right side of the trail, as promised by Casebier; I knew I was on the right trail. The road was a sandy path that led across a wide valley to the **Piute Mountains**.

This area was the western edge of the Mojave Indians' territory. They would pass through here on their way to the coast to trade, but from Piute Valley westward we were in the land of the Chemehuevis and Piute Indians. These tribes were unfriendly with the Mojaves,

Mojave Desert

and didn't take well to the Americans, either. They commenced hostilities against the Americans when the numbers grew from a trickle to a flood, and when prospectors started hunting the strange gold rocks on their desert. That's where the five military installations come in; they were established to keep the watering holes secure and protect the mail and the travelers. Whoever controls the water controls the desert.

The first stop is **Fort Piute**. A day's wagon drive from the Colorado River, Piute Springs is on the eastern slope of the Piute Mountains. It was a long haul – mostly uphill – from the river, a full day's work to get there by wagon. But it only took me a half-hour from Highway 95, mostly in four-wheel-drive because of the sand. The fort was just where Dennis Casebier's book told me it would be; around a cinder-cone known as Jed Smith Hill, next to a creek that was all of two feet wide but running strong.

Fort Piute

Stone foundations remain to mark the site of the fort, as well as the remains of a ranch from the 1940s just downstream from the old fort.

Fort Piute was never really a fort, according to the US Army. It was an outpost, called a "redoubt," housing 18 enlisted men whose job was to occupy the land around the spring and the creek so the Indians couldn't. Without a supply of water, hostile forces could not operate in the vicinity, and the wagons making their way westward would be safer from attack.

The early travelers would continue westward up the canyon from the fort but, due to changes in the land since that time, we have to backtrack and go around the mountain and the gorge. Desert storms have washed out the trail here and made it impassable for vehicles. It was on this backtrack that I learned once again that the rules of desert travel should not be ignored.

I'd driven only a half-hour from the highway, but it was a fairly good four-wheeling road; rough and rocky in places, heavy sand in others, but not low-range tough. It was a good eight miles, which would be a three-hour walk and heavy work in the deep sand – the sort of fact one keeps in mind when heading out in open country. But when the Jeep stalled out on a tough climb out of Piute Creek, I wasn't worried, until I realized the front wheels were not engaged. Behind me was deep sand. Even if I could get out of the rocks I was in, I'd probably not be able to pass through the sand without four-wheel drive. But God looks out for children and fools and salvation was on the trail behind me, in the form of Dave Hughes and his Chevy Suburban.

Dave and his Chevy in Piute Creek.

Dave, a businessman from Hesperia, owns an auto repair shop and has built his Suburban into a fine off-highway trail runner. A lift kit and 35-inch tires gives it a lot of clearance, and the 460 hp engine he put in, with the winch on the front bumper lets him tow any number of little Jeep Cherokees out of danger. No four-wheeler wants to be towed out. But I wasn't going to object to a little help.

Dave walked up and we kicked a few rocks out of the way, and after discussing the problem we backed the Jeep into the sand. I popped open the hood and Dave started following vacuum lines, then crawled underneath my rig and re-attached the line that controls the front wheel drive. I was back in business, and climbed out of the riverbed easily. Dave, who knew the rules of desert travel as well or better than I do, was heading in the same direction and for the same reasons, so we traveled on together.

To cross the Piute Mountains, we must go around to the **Cable Road** and take a low pass. The Cable Road was built to maintain the underground telephone line that was buried here during the days of the Cold War. This is a beautiful pass and, as the road slowly climbs over the Piutes, splendid vistas appear along the way, in every direction. The Cable Road drops us down into the Joshua-covered plain of Lanfair Valley where we rejoin the Mojave Road.

Cholla cactus along Cable Road, near Fort Piute.

Marks of the past scar **Lanfair**. During the early 1900s the desert went through a wet period, and settlers attempted to farm the valley. They ripped out acres and acres of Joshua trees to plant crops that didn't belong here. The dry environment defeated the farmers, but the marks of their efforts remain in the empty fields. These patches won't be fully reclaimed for hundreds of years as the Joshua grows very slowly. But in the parts of the valley where the scars of man are hidden, the forests are splendid and plentiful and the Mojave Road winds through them. At times the trail is two or three feet below the surface of the surrounding land due to erosion, and the road is made of a powder sand that grabs your wheels and tries to pull you in. Off the sides of the road there are random signs of people: an old bus that may have been someone's home at some time in the distant past; a trailer or motor home parked off in the distance; a cabin built of rock; and an Omni navigation station used by aircraft. These things are remarkable only because we had seen almost nothing else to remind us of civilization, and we had traveled a good 30 miles.

We stop to rest and stretch and examine an old piece of mining gear. It's an A-frame with wooden doors attached at the bottom. It probably went over a deep shaft, and the top of the A-frame was used with a block and tackle to lift the rock out of the diggings. It's old, desert-old, but still usable.

A few miles after crossing the Ivanpah-Lanfair Road, a nicely maintained and graded dirt road, the trail begins to climb and the terrain gradually changes. We are beginning to see more piñon and juniper here as the elevation approaches 5,000 feet. We are approaching two important stops on the Mojave Road: Rock Spring and Government Holes. **Rock Spring** was the next watering station for the wagons, and it is a pleasant little spot in a rock canyon between the mountains. **Government Holes** is about two miles down the trail.

The Gunfight at Government Holes

Government Holes (also known as Government Wells) has a colorful history. It's the site of one the last confrontations between cattlemen and farmers, a stereotype of the Old West , with big ranchers and small farmers fighting for the watering holes. It's also the site of one of the last classic gunfights. But neither the gunfight nor the cattle war took place in the 1800s. They occurred in 1925.

J.W. "Bill" Robinson was a gunfighter, hired by a cattle company to keep the water sources open for their cattle.

Whoever controlled water here also controlled huge amounts of land; both were needed to keep cattle or corn alive. So Robinson was stationed at Government Holes to keep it open for cattle.

Matt Burts was also a gunfighter, and had worked for cattle interests in the past, but presently he was living in Lanfair Valley and was involved with the farming interests there. There was talk in the valley that Robinson had been hired to kill Burts, and much discussion took place over which was the better man with a gun. This talk probably helped fuel the competitive fire between the men, and they chose to end the discussion when they met up on November 8, 1925.

Casebier, in his *Mojave Road Guide*, says it went down this way: "On that day, a Sunday, Matt Burts arrived at Government Holes in a Model T in company with a Mrs. L. A. Riedel and her grandson, Charles Harold Fulton. Robinson was in the cabin. Burts yelled into the cabin saying they needed water for the car. Robinson yelled back his acknowledgement and approval. Then he invited Burts inside while Mrs. Riedel and her grandson tended to the car.

"Mrs. Riedel heard voices inside and then a terrible noise. The gunfighters had each emptied their .45s into one another." Both men were killed.

By the time we reached Government Holes, we'd traveled 40 miles on dirt, mostly in four-wheel-drive. Ahead was Marl Springs, a place I must get to, but even I had had about enough trail-riding for one day. After seven hours of off-highway travel every bone in the body feels shaken down. We picked up the Cedar Canyon Road – a superhighway, after the trail, even if it isn't paved. Dave was heading for the Mid Hills Campground for a night in the piñon high country. I directed the Jeep down the hill and back to the interstate, feeling I had earned a night in a comfortable motel.

Heading down **Cedar Canyon**, more breathtaking vistas unfolded. The Mid Hills and the Providence Mountains pointed southward beyond Kelso. The Kelso Dunes lay gloriously at their feet, a white streak that pointed west to the sandy expanse of the Devil's Playground. Ahead were the Beale and Marl Mountains, and to the north of them, the Cima Dome rose curiously to fill the space between the Ivanpahs and the Beales. In the foreground, a railroad track incongruously split the scene, and a long freight train moaned its way up the steep bajada to Cima. A fitting sight to end the day.

The next time I was on the Mojave Road was several weeks later. My desert-dancing trail partner Suz was along. We'd spent a delightful morning at Goffs with Dennis Casebier, then headed northward to Cedar Canyon and the Cima Road. There, we picked up the trail and headed west. Suz drove; she'd been cooped up in civilization too long and needed the time on the trail. The trail lay before us, with not a single other mark of man within sight. We were in a magnificent Joshua tree forest. A falcon hunted in the sky above, soaring and sailing and keeping a sharp eye on the desert floor for his dinner. The road was rough, very rough, from washouts, and sandy washes kept us in four-wheel-drive as we made our way toward the Beale Mountains. We slowed to one or two miles an hour; jostling easily along, with no sign of the 20th century around us; we were a wagon heading westward on the interminable trail to the golden land of California.

We moseyed along, watching for dancing Joshuas and wild horses or burros; Casebier said this was a prime area for them. To our right was the unusual Cima Dome, but we were on the side of it and its dome shape was not discernible. The Beale Mountains slowly passed us by and we began the long march to the Marls. This is truly empty country; not another soul was in sight. But now the marks of our time came into view. A power line from Boulder Dam to Los Angeles appeared as we approached the Marl Mountains.

Marl Springs

The Marls were named by Army lieutenant Amiel Weeks Whipple. He was here on March 7, 1854, with a survey party. He gave the springs the name, which later became associated with the mountains, because of the "marly" soil around the springs; it is a type of clay that, when wet, clings and slips like caliche, a sediment often found in desert regions.

Mojave Desert

The springs make a beautiful high desert oasis. The lower springs are fenced to hold cattle, but the gate is left open most of the time. A tank is full of wonderful water, cold and fresh. This is the gathering place for desert animals from miles around; wild horses, burros, coyotes, desert foxes, and so much more take full advantage of the improvements made by the cattlemen to this ancient watering hole.

Ancient Watering Hole.

Indian Attack!

For a short time – from October 5, 1867 through May 22, 1868 – the Army stationed a few soldiers at Marl Springs. On October 17, three men – Sgt. Thomas Johnston (who was in charge of the detachment), Pvt. John Ahern, and Pvt. Jackson Thompson, all of Company "K," 14th US Infantry, were building a stone corral at the upper spring when a band of 20 to 30 Indians attacked. All three men made it to safety inside their stone headquarters, but the Indians laid siege to the outpost. They continued through the night, and in the morning, the soldiers were rescued in classic Western storybook style: A column of 150 soldiers came over the hill and the Indians scattered.

While standing at the upper spring, with the crystal-clear view eastward and the Marl Mountains behind, it isn't hard at all to hear the war cries of the attacking Indians. I hear the angry bark of the rifles and pistols, feel the rush of an arrow skimming by, and taste the terror of imminent death as we run to the remains of the stone redoubt. We feel the incredible joy of just being alive, and the dread as night slowly but inexorably approaches: what will the Indians do? Will they leave as they came, silently and without any hint? Everyone must stay alert as the long night drags on. Feel the relief as the desert night slowly changes to false dawn, and the yellow and reds appear in the eastern sky; then the sun slowly rises, the column of soldiers marches in – and the hostiles fade into the desert.

The Army occupied this area for only a few months, but Marl Springs was an important stop along the Mojave Road for all of its lifetime. It is a distant 30 miles from Marl to the next watering hole westward – **Soda Springs**, now called Zzyzx – and it was a long, hard journey by wagon. The road passes through the heavy sands of the **Devil's Playground**, crosses the **Mojave River Sink**, and takes us through **Soda Lake** before watering up at Soda Springs. And the water at Soda Springs was brackish at best, barely tolerable at worst.

So Marl was, and is, important, as the only water source for many miles. During the wagon trail days, several different civilians operated stations here, where they could sell travelers a fresh-cooked meal, some grain for their horses, and a place to sleep. Prospectors worked out of here as well; near the upper spring is a well-preserved arrastra, a crude piece of equipment once used to crush rock for extracting gold. The springs have always been a headquarters for the cattle industry. Now, no one lives (or camps) near the springs as that would keep the half-wild cattle and native animals away from them.

Proceeding westward on the road, we found ourselves in a uniquely beautiful area. The road reaches a summit, and the expanse of the lower Mojave – the Devil's Playground, Cave Mountain, and Soda Lake – are at our feet. It is breathtaking, one more beautiful view in a land filled with beautiful views. We are indeed on top of the world here, in the heart of the wilderness, and forever stretches all around us.

Mojave Desert

But the winter day was waning; winter nights are bitter cold here, and driving on desert trails in the dark is a particularly difficult venture. It was time to head back to civilization. We made our way to pavement in the glow of sunset, and reluctantly left Dennis Casebier's road behind.

We'd be back. This trail is too special to be away from it for long.

If You Go

The wonderful Mojave Road starts at the Colorado River near Laughlin, Nevada, and ends in Afton Canyon near Barstow. Before going, get a copy of Dennis Casebier's Mojave Road Guide, and read it over carefully. Then bring it with you – it's invaluable.

Be sure to take along maps as well. A good recreation map of the Mojave National Preserve is published by Tom Harrison (☎ 800-265-9090). But don't rely on maps alone for driving the Mojave Road. This is not an easy trip and it should not be undertaken lightly. Remember what Dennis Casebier says: You can die out there.

The section of trail that I traveled in the first part of this chapter (pages 76-83) is 48 miles, which I covered in seven hours, including numerous stops. It is definitely four-wheel-drive only. Much of it would be rated as easy, but parts require good clearance as well as low gears. The second part of the trail is shorter – about 20 miles – but still a several-hour excursion, and it's a long way from pavement or services. We saw no other people along this section of the trail, and no sign that anyone had been on it in weeks.

The trail crosses Highway 95 about 25 miles south of Searchlight. The trail can also be easily found on the Cima-Kelso Road, south of Cima, across from the Cedar Canyon Road. The Clampers, a Western social club formerly known as E. Clampus Vitus, have erected a monument at this point.

The rock cairns built by the Friends of the Mojave Trail are very helpful. They are always on the right when traveling west.

It bears repeating: Be prepared for trouble here; it is a long, long way to help. Take extra water and food, and double-check your emergency supplies, tools and tires before taking off. Stay on the road to avoid getting stuck or damaging the scenery for the next people to travel the road behind you.

There is dispersed camping, and a nice campground (no phone) at Mid Hills in the preserve. Accommodations can be found in Baker, Barstow, Searchlight, Laughlin, and Primm, Nevada. Primm is just across the state line on Interstate 15 and has three Las Vegas-style resort hotels with cheap rooms and cheap, good food.

Mojave Desert

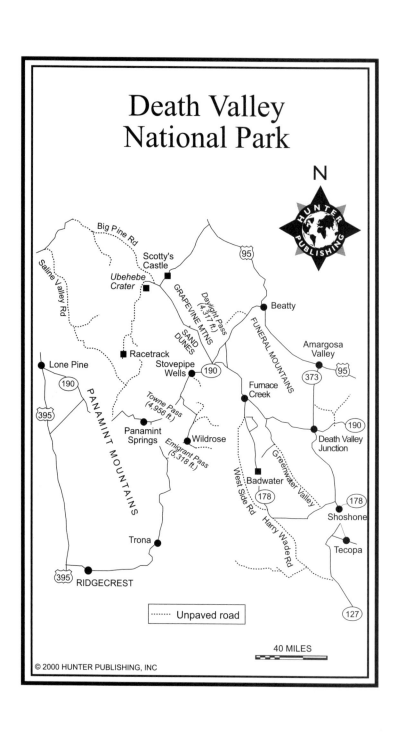

Death Valley
National Park

N

Big Pine Rd

Scotty's Castle

Ubehebe Crater

Saline Valley Rd

GRAPEVINE MTNS

Daylight Pass (4,317 ft.)

95

Beatty

SAND DUNES

FUNERAL MOUNTAINS

Amargosa Valley

Racetrack

Stovepipe Wells

190

Furnace Creek

373

95

Lone Pine

190

Towne Pass (4,956 ft.)

PANAMINT MOUNTAINS

395

Panamint Springs

Wildrose

Emigrant Pass (5,318 ft.)

Greenwater Valley

190

Death Valley Junction

West Side Rd

Badwater

178

Harry Wade Rd

178

Shoshone

Trona

Tecopa

395 RIDGECREST

⋯⋯⋯ Unpaved road

40 MILES

127

Death Valley

Introduction

For many years I avoided Death Valley. It wasn't the desert I loved; it was a parody of the desert, a desert gone Hollywood. Nothing about it was easy to like or to understand. It's famous for terrible suffering, with great odds against survival. Its very name is dreadful: Death Valley. These words conjure visions of legends, of men bigger than life, tackling a frontier so wildly strange that the moon seems more hospitable.

I didn't like it, I didn't understand it, but I had to go see if it was real. When we finally bit the bullet and pushed the Jeep over Towne's Pass and down the hill to Furnace Creek, I fell in love. It still isn't real to me and I still don't understand it; but I love it, and I'm learning.

Richard Lingenfelter, in his wonderful book, *Death Valley and the Amargosa*, calls this area the land of illusions. He's right; nature runs amok here. It is a geographical oddity, one of the hottest places on earth, and one of the most eerily beautiful.

To call it a valley is like calling Los Angeles a community. It is a huge and deep valley, 170 miles long and a mile to two miles deep. It is a land of extremes. While standing at its lowest point (282 feet below sea level), the majestic peaks of the Panamint Mountains rise nearby to an elevation of more than 11,000 feet. Often they are covered with snow.

>>━━━━━━━━━━━━━━━━━━━━━━━━━━━━━━━━<<

A Land of Extremes

From a point in the Panamints, looking eastward you can see Badwater in the heart of Death Valley, which is the lowest point in the United States; to the west you can see Mt. McKinley, the highest mountain in the contiguous US.

Death Valley is incredibly hot, incredibly strange, and very inhospitable. It is the second hottest place on earth. It misses being the hottest by only two degrees; the official record is 134° in Death Valley, and 136° in the Libyan Sahara.

>>━━━━━━━━━━━━━━━━━━━━━━━━━━━━━━━━<<

Despite the conditions, humans have made Death Valley home for hundreds of years. Native Americans – the **Timbesha Shoshone tribe** – adapted well to the unique environment, usually spending the summer at a camp in the mountains, then moving down into the valley for a nice, warm winter. About a hundred or so of the tribe still live in the valley today.

In the early 20th century, numerous prospectors, scientists, one notable con artist, and a semi-retired businessman made Death Valley their home. These people spent many years learning the secrets of this strange land and living lives that were so large they still amaze (and in some cases, amuse) us. Chinese laborers dug borax from the floor of a dry lakebed, where the surface of the ground reaches as high as 170°. And thanks to the modern miracle of air conditioning, today several hundred people make Death Valley their home, serving the tourists that come to experience this strange and barren land.

From the Panamints to the Amargosa

A nd strange this land is. There's a place in Death Valley where the rocks move, seemingly on their own. They leave tracks as they scoot around on a dry lakebed known as The Racetrack. Scientists say this probably happens when the lake gets a little rain, followed by stiff winds; the rain mixes with the soil of the lakebed, making an extremely slick surface, and the rocks move with the wind. Either that, or some very big and strong ghosts work here. No one has ever seen the rocks move; all anyone ever sees is the tracks the rocks leave behind.

Nearby is **Ubehebe Crater**, a volcano that erupted just an eyeblink ago in geological time. Just 4,000 years ago there was a massive explosion when rising magma encountered a layer of groundwater, blowing the top off the mountain and leaving a pit a half-mile wide and 500 feet deep. A smaller crater close to Ubehebe erupted a mere 1,000 years ago.

Ubehebe Crater.

In the heart of Death Valley there stands a plain known as the Devil's Cornfield. That's what it looks like, too; stalks of corn bunched together, standing tall, clumped in orderly formations. The oldest rocks on earth are in the valley – as is a scarp formed during an earthquake just a few years ago.

A geographical oddity, certainly. It is a land of stark contrasts with the old and new standing side by side. Plants and animals found no-where else in the world have adapted to living through the incredible dry heat of a Death Valley summer; others live well in the foul brine of its water.

The First Travelers

Aside from a few mountain men and explorers, a wandering party of '49ers were the first group from the American states to see Death Valley. They'd turned south at Salt Lake to avoid the Sierras and the fate of the Donner Party. Their shock and dismay at first seeing the threatening, dry expanse of Death Valley and the wall of mountains beyond can only be imagined. While crossing the valley each person fought a terrible battle for survival, with each man for himself, strug-gling to escape the horrible heat and deprivation. It is from this party that Death Valley got its name.

These first white-American tourists came to Death Valley because they'd tarried too long on the trail to California. They had arrived in Salt Lake City too late to make it over the Sierras before snowfall closed the pass. In Salt Lake, they heard stories of the **Old Spanish Trail**, a path that led between New Mexico and the pueblo at Los Angeles. They sought out guides to this trail, and the wagons headed south into hell.

The stories of their trip across the deserts of Utah, Nevada, and Cali-fornia have grown into legends. This group was by no means a cohe-sive unit; they were casual acquaintances, with no loyalty to each other and one goal uppermost in each person's mind: to get to Cali-fornia. Even more, each wanted to get to the goldfields before all the gold was gone, and to get there ahead of the others. It was a race and, while their common sense kept them together for protection and mu-tual support, their greed and sometimes outright stupidity drove them apart.

Long before they entered what would come to be known as Death Valley the wagon train had split into factions. One group stayed with the wagonmaster and continued south to the old Spanish Trail, which circumvented most of Death Valley. This group fared much better than the people who went searching for a middle crossing of the Sierras and who entered Death Valley to face the two-mile-high wall of the Panamint Mountains.

Truth & Fiction

This wagon train became a leading feature in a dime novel published years later, the tale of a train of 80 or so wagons and 400 emigrants, all of whom died while crossing Death Valley. This story was complete fiction. As far as anyone can determine, only one person from that wagon train died in Death Valley. Most of the wagons were indeed lost, either abandoned or chopped into two-wheel carts that handled the rough terrain much more efficiently. But the sensational story of a lost wagon train created the myth of a valley of death that haunts the area today.

The fact that the legend of death and a lost wagon train is false, or that only one victim died in the valley that would become famous for its deadly threat, should not minimize the hell these '49ers went through. The real story, of weeks of wandering, starvation, thirst, deprivation, and the horrible fear of being lost in a strange, inhospitable land is a remarkable one. The lost wagon train was just the first of many tales that would be spread about Death Valley.

The Lost Gunsight Mine

Another tale tells of a '49er named Jim Martin, who picked up a rock he recognized as pure silver while wandering through one of the many mountain ranges. He carried the rock with him all the way to Mariposa in the Sierras, where he had it made into a gunsight for his rifle. This piece of silver fired the imagination of Rainbow Seekers everywhere, and the search for the Lost Gunsight mine became a quest that has lasted for 150 years.

Death Valley

There are many, many other legends that were born in and around Death Valley. Some of the most fantastic stock frauds ever perpetrated were initiated here, during the big mining booms of the early 1900s. The world's most famous con man lived here, Death Valley Scotty, who got away with nearly every scam he pulled, and lived in a castle built by one of his victims. Because of the aura surrounding Death Valley, he was able to get away with such outrageous behavior and subsequently became an American icon. He fed the legends, and became one, because the land here is bigger than life.

So this is the land of telltales. Enjoy them, but don't take the stories too seriously. Certainly don't let them interfere with your enjoyment of the land. For this is one of the most magnificent desert areas in the world, a land of startling contrasts, wonderful acts of nature, and serene vistas.

A Visit to the Racetrack

Of all the places in Death Valley, this one grabbed my attention the most. Yes, the valley floor is beautiful, but ever since I'd heard about the rocks that move I knew I had to go see them.

Our expedition to the Racetrack began on one of the most glorious spring days we'd seen; the sun was bright, but the weather was not yet uncomfortably warm. Distant thin clouds promised not to bring any rain, just a little welcome shade perhaps. The wind was a mild breeze; the wind can be as much an enemy as the sun but today it would stay light and easy. It was a perfect day for a long trip on sand and gravel.

Getting to the Racetrack isn't easy. Predictably, I chose the most difficult route to get there, a four-wheeling expedition that equals or surpasses any I've ever taken. It was a white-knuckle cliff-hanger, and Suz says I'd better enjoy the memory; we're never going back. Dally agrees with her, enforcing her opinion with a growl.

It's located beyond Ubehebe Crater, which is north of Scotty's Castle. The National Park Service advises that four-wheel drive may be needed to get to the Racetrack. Coming around from the north, by Ubehebe Crater, I think they're wrong; the road is washboarded but graded and easy, usually fit for the family sedan. Coming from the south, however, is an entirely different story.

There are two ways through from the south. One is a relatively easy four-wheeling trail. The second route is a detour off of the first, up the serious, high-pucker-factor, mountain-goat trail known as the **Lippincott Mine Road**. Of course, that's the road we chose.

Looking down on the Lippincott Mine Road.

Both trails take off from the **Saline Valley Road** north of State Highway 190, which is north of Darwin and west of Panamint Springs. There are no road signs; not even BLM markers. The Saline Valley Road is paved, for a ways; but it's old, not maintained, and only a single lane wide. It's really just one long pothole, until it finally turns to dirt.

The road climbs out of the saline flats and up into cattle country, through Joshua forests into cedar and juniper, and finally dusty pines. We broke out into the open and found ourselves on the edge of a mountain, looking southward toward the Panamints. The 11,000-foot Telescope Peak was in snowbound glory, and a few miles away we could almost see the mud houses of Ballarat at about 2,000 feet on the edge of the playa.

The road rounded the mountain, and we were facing the Inyos, about as high as the Panamints, with the floor of Saline Valley spread before us. We followed Saline Valley Road down past chocolate-colored rock upthrusts and dropped quickly to the flats.

At the intersection of the Saline Valley Road with the Lippincott Mine Road (on some maps, Lippincott is identified as the Ubehebe Crater Road) there's a large rock cairn, and just beyond a sign that warms the heart of any dedicated four-wheeler.

It says: "Caution. Route ahead not maintained. Washouts and cut banks ahead. Route not recommended for vehicle travel. Experienced drivers using 4x4 high clearance vehicles only."

As it turns out, they're not kidding.

The trail rounds the foot of a mountain, then heads up a canyon that winds its way through spectacular scenery. The rocks are a collage of granite, sedimentary conglomerates, and a lot of interesting quartz – gold-bearing, perhaps, judging from the amount of mining and the number of prospect holes in the canyon.

The climb gets very serious – almost straight up, it seems. This is slow, low-range work. There are washouts, most of which have been repaired with rocks, and in places you'll only have a foot or so between your outside tire and a disaster. The drop gets hairy: hundreds of feet – not straight down, but close to it. A mistake could be fatal.

There's an additional problem: the breeze in the canyon is blowing from behind. We're in a low-range, high-RPM climb, moving at perhaps four or five miles an hour. Even though it isn't a hot day – in the 80s – the Jeep's engine starts to heat up. We have to stop twice to let things cool down. Finally the road tops out at a saddle. This isn't the summit, but it's a good stopping point, and the view westward is fantastic as the Saline Valley lies at your feet. There's room to park with the grill facing into the wind to let things cool.

Farther on, the pucker-factor eases as the dropoffs are not as severe, but the trail remains a challenge with switchbacks and washouts and low-range climbs. The trail ends just beyond the summit at a nice bladed road, with another warning sign like the first for the traffic coming from the other direction. Beyond is the Racetrack, and 28 miles of gravel to Ubehebe.

The Racetrack is not an illusion. The rocks really do move.

Hiking out onto the playa, we examine the soil of the lakebed. It is indeed a very fine material, and I could imagine how slick it would become when wet. According to the Park Service's sign, the winds here hit 70 mph or more. Surely that is enough force to push these rocks around.

No one has ever seen them move. After all these years, a hundred or more since this phenomena was brought to the attention of the naturalists studying Death Valley, no one has seen the rocks move.

A rock leaves its trail at the Racetrack.

The rocks come from a formation to the north called the Grandstand, and from a ridge on the east across the lake. They aren't boulders; they are rocks, up to perhaps a foot or so tall. The rocks are spread out on the lake and we walk from one to another. Most had no trails, no sign at all of anything unusual.

But some rocks farther north did not let us down. The trail in the dry playa was clear; this rock had moved a substantial distance without human or animal help; there were no tracks around it, no record of assistance, just the path it made as it slid through the mud. It had changed directions, several times. It was easy to see the record of various windstorms, and imagine how long they lasted; some a short time, some for days, with wind coming from different directions that made the rock slide in different ways.

We found more, some with tracks around them, from people who had walked out on the playa while the mud was still wet. That would have been interesting, to be here when the lake bed was still moist, and experience the soil conditions. I'd be tempted to wait for the wind and try to catch the rocks shifting. But this would be one miserable place in a storm with 70 mph winds, and surely others have tried, without success, to catch the rocks in the act.

On second thought, the wind may not be the culprit. I think it's the ghosts of the Rainbow Seekers playing a trick on us.

If You Go

Winter or spring is the best time to visit Death Valley. Since it's the second-hottest place in the world (only the Sahara is hotter), summer should be avoided if you want to do anything but sit by an air conditioner. Winter weather in the Valley is moderate, but be fully prepared for all kinds of weather in nearby areas. There's always the chance of a snowstorm if you go exploring in the Panamints or other nearby mountains.

There is a $10 fee per vehicle to enter the park. The fee is good for a week.

The park is best explored by private vehicle. A four-wheel-drive with good clearance is recommended for tours in the Panamints and to the Racetrack. Keep a full gas tank. It's a big park, there are only three locations where you can get gas, and you'll drive much farther than you might expect.

*The main **visitor center** is at Furnace Creek near the junction of California Routes 178 and 190. The center is open daily, summer and winter.*

Ranger stations and information stations are located at the Wildrose Campground, Route 178 at the west end of the park; Stovepipe Wells on Route 190; in Shoshone, near the junction of California Routes 178 and 127; and in Beatty, on Route 374 near US Route 95. ☎ (760) 786-2331.

*There are two places in the park to get **food and supplies**: at Furnace Creek and Stovepipe Wells. Gas is available there and at Scotty's Castle. Furnace Creek also has the **Borax Museum**, ☎ (760) 786-2345, and there are bookstores at Scotty's Castle, Furnace Creek, and Stovepipe Wells.*

Death Valley Lodging

Hotels & Motels

There are two resorts in Death Valley, at Furnace Creek and Stovepipe Wells. For reservation information write to Fred Harvey, Inc., PO Box 187, Death Valley, CA 92328, or call the **Furnace Creek Inn** at ☎ 760-786-2361 or the **Furnace Creek Ranch** at ☎ 760-786-2345. At the **Stovepipe Wells Village** there is a motel and limited camping facilities. ☎ 760-786-2387 for information.

Near the Panamint Mountains west of the valley, the **Panamint Springs Resort** is a hotel and resort campground. Their phone number is ☎ 702-482-7680.

No other lodging is available within the park, and from May to October services in all areas may be limited or reduced. Accommodations outside of the park are a long distance away – this is a very remote area. The nearest communities with hotels are:

- ◈ Baker, California – 60 miles south
- ◈ Ridgecrest, California – 70 miles southwest
- ◈ Barstow, California – 120 miles south
- ◈ Beatty, Nevada – 15 miles east
- ◈ Las Vegas, Nevada – 85 miles east

Death Valley

Camping

In addition to dispersed camping in many areas, there are nine campgrounds in the park. Only three of them are open year-round: Furnace Creek, Mesquite Spring, and Wildrose. Three are open between October and April: Texas Spring, Sunset, and Stovepipe Wells. Three other campgrounds are open from April to October: Emigrant, Thorndike, and Mahogany. Camping fees range from $10 to $16.

For dispersed camping, check with a park ranger to find out where this is allowed. Dispersed camping is not allowed on the road between The Racetrack and Scotty's Castle.

Primitive camping is allowed in the backcountry areas, but check at the ranger station for details. Also, obtain a camping permit from the rangers. Generally, camping is allowed two miles back from main paved or unpaved roads and within a quarter-mile of water sources.

Roadside camping is not permitted. Campfires are allowed only in fireplaces and portable stoves. Camping is limited to no more than 30 days per year throughout the park. Camping limits are 14 days at Furnace Creek Campground and 30 days at all others.

Call Death Valley National Park, ☎ 760-786-2331, for more information on these campgrounds. In addition, you can call ☎ 800-365-2267 to reserve campsites in all of the national parks.

Furnace Creek has over 100 sites. It is located north of the visitor center on Route 190; elevation is 196 feet below sea level. Fee $16.

Texas Spring is open in the winter and has 92 sites. It is south of the visitor center off Route 190; sea level elevation. Fee $10.

Sunset is the largest campground, with 1,000 sites. It is open in winter. It is south of the visitor center off Route 190; elevation 190 feet below sea level. Fee $10.

Stovepipe Wells has 200 sites. It is north of Stovepipe Wells, off Route 190; sea level elevation. Fee $10.

Emigrant is a small campground, only 10 sites, open during the summer. It is on the west side of the park at the fork of Routes 190 and 178; elevation 2,100 feet. No fee.

Mesquite Spring has 30 sites and is open year-round. It is at the north end of the park, west of Route 267; elevation 1,800 feet. Fee $10.

Wildrose is accessible only with a four-wheel-drive vehicle. It has 30 sites and is open year-round. It is in Wildrose Canyon – the former outlaw hangout of the 1800s – on the western edge of the park, just off Route 178. The elevation is 4,100 feet. No fee charged.

Thorndike is another four-wheel-drive campground, with only eight sites, open in summer, and located near Wildrose. The elevation is 7,500 feet. No fee is charged.

Mahogany Flat is also a four-wheel-drive camp in the Panamints with 10 sites, open in summer. The elevation is 8,200 feet. No fee is charged.

Remember that this is a national park – so no shooting or hunting is allowed; animals, rocks, plants, artifacts, and fossils must be left undisturbed. Don't feed or try to handle any wild animals. All vehicles (including bicycles) must remain on designated trails. No loaded firearms are allowed. Pets must be leashed or confined at all times.

Safety Precautions

Death Valley is famous for losing tourists to the incredible heat, the vast distances, and overconfidence – don't overestimate your abilities or underestimate the dangers of the desert. Read the *Appendix* in this book and follow the precautions religiously.

◈ Never travel the deserted trails alone. Always tell someone where you are going and when you expect to be back. If it looks like rain, stay out of arroyos and canyons.

◈ There are a number of abandoned mines, and they can be dangerous places. There may be vertical shafts, or unstable supports that could cave in; either condition could kill you. Sometimes there are caches of dynamite that were left behind – report any you find to the nearest ranger, and leave it alone.

◈ Carry plenty of water (at least one gallon per person per day) and drink it. Most desert deaths here are from dehydration, not heat exhaustion. Saving your drinking water until later is not recommended. Drink it before your body needs it.

◈ If your vehicle breaks down, stay with it. It is much easier to find a vehicle than a wandering person. Also, distances are deceiving on the desert. An object that appears to be just a mile or two distant may be 10 or 20 miles away.

Beatty Sidetrip

If you go, don't miss the wonderful Nevada town of **Beatty**. *It's a typical Western town, with easygoing, friendly people who don't mind helping out a stranger. I broke down there once, on the way to The Racetrack, and the folks at the Burro Inn and the local NAPA store went beyond the call of duty to get this stranger back on the road. I appreciated their Western hospitality and assistance, which they offered as a matter of course, but I saw as a great act of kindness.*

You don't have to break down there to enjoy Beatty. But if you do, look up Roger (the maintenance man at The Burro Inn) and I'll bet he'll get you on your way.

There's a great little museum, and a helpful lady who is a goldmine of information at the Death Valley Visitor's Center. Don't miss **Rhyolite**, *either, as it's just down the road.*

From Beatty to Ballarat

Beatty, Nevada, is nestled between desert mountains along the main route between Las Vegas and Reno. It's the eastern entrance to Death Valley, which gives it some tourist trade; otherwise, the town lives off mining and cows. It is a Western town filled with easygoing, hardworking people.

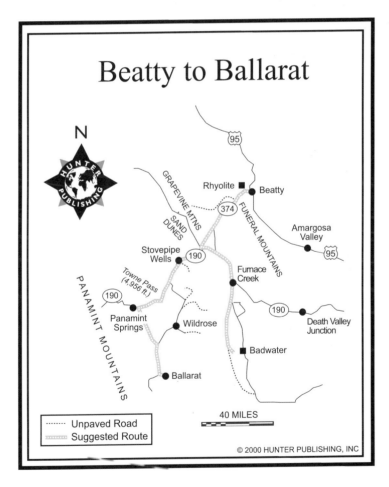

"Nothing much ever happens here," said the young lady at the registration desk at the Burro Inn. The Burro Inn is an older place, a Nevada-style motel with a restaurant and casino that is open 24 hours. There's a wooden Indian outside the door to the restaurant, a friendly-looking character in full Native American dress and with a bent nose. He belongs. Beatty is a step back in time, a quiet little town. It's a wide spot on the edge of nowhere, and in the spirit of young people everywhere, whose juices are flowing and whose questing spirit is yearning for experience and adventure, our clerk would rather be where there was some excitement.

But excitement is just what Beatty was all about a hundred years ago, when just over the hill in the Bullfrog district tent cities arose with the speed of a flash flood. Gold was found, and thousands of prospectors and camp followers arrived.

On the Trail of Shorty Harris

Shorty Harris was part of it from the beginning. It was his strike, with his partner Ernest Cross, that touched off the run to the Bullfrogs, and created the town of Rhyolite, Nevada. Located over the hill and a few miles west of Beatty, Rhyolite and a few other camps sprang up almost overnight and became the sensation of Death Valley when the boys found gold in a green rock in August 1904.

Shorty Harris is a name that is heard all over Death Valley. He was a controversial character at times, perhaps a little loose with the truth, a single-blanket-jackass-prospector with a taste for whiskey and a habit of spending a little too much time with a bottle of O, Be Joyful. He was born Frank Harris in Rhode Island in 1857, and was an orphan at the tender age of seven. In the 1870s he rode the rails west to make his fortune, and spent time in mining camps from Leadville to Tombstone and the Idaho country, before coming to Death Valley. He stood all of five feet, four inches tall; he had big ears, sparkling blue eyes and a bushy moustache. He usually had to wear pants and coats that were too big for him.

And, he was an exceptionally good prospector. He could find gold the way some people catch colds. Over his lifetime in Death Valley, he'd found many a good claim, but he would sell them to someone else who had the resources and the desire to develop them. Shorty would take his fee, go out on a binge, spend all the money then return to his desert and start all over again.

He was popular, the kind of man would give a stranger the shirt off his back. Many old-timers had been fed or tanked up by Shorty when he was in the chips, and they'd return the favor anytime he needed it. He always had a partner, whether it was while prospecting or while he was out on a drinking spree. Shorty loved to talk, and he loved the conviviality of saloons much more than the hard labor of mucking ore. The veracity of his stories might be open to question – truth wasn't his strong point, and most of his stories made him out to be quite a hero – but he was well-liked in spite of that.

Bullfrog was his first and best strike. The gold was pure, veins of gorgeous color in a green rock that reminded Shorty of bullfrogs; hence the name.

In 1904, the Bullfrog Mountains were just some unnamed dry hills west of Montillus Murray Beatty's ranch, which he had established about a quarter-century before. Shorty was taking part in the excitement at Goldfield some 80 miles north of Beatty's ranch. But no good locations were left at Goldfield – he had arrived at the strike too late to find a claim worth having. So he headed over to the Funeral Mountains where his friend Jack Keane had made a good strike.

There, at Keane's Wonder mine, he found himself once again on the outside looking in; there were dozens of prospects but no good locations left unclaimed that had any sign of gold. Shorty remembered some hills to the east in which he had seen some good indications. Cross, who was also coming up empty at the Keane strike, partnered with Shorty and they headed out.

He told the story of the discovery to a newspaperman (from the *Rhyolite Herald*) a few years later in 1909:

> "We packed the four burros and struck out, together with some other prospectors who had joined in the Keane Wonder rush. Some of the boys went to Thorp's and some to Tokop, but when we came to Daylight Springs I told Cross I had passed up a country some time before, and as it looked good to me, we

Death Valley

would go back to it. We came on to Buck Springs.

"Next morning we started west. Cross started down to the little hill to the south, and I went over to the blowout. I found lots of quartz all over the hill and started to break it with my pick. Cross hadn't moved over 400 feet away when I called him back.

"I had run against a boulder, and I called out, 'Come back, we've got it!'

"The quartz was just full of free gold, and it was the original genuine green Bullfrog rock. Talk about rich! Why, gee whiz, it was great! We took the stuff back to the spring and panned it, and we certainly went straight up. The very first boulder was as rich in gold as anything I had ever seen."

That was Shorty's story of the discovery, but Cross's version varied somewhat. About 40 years later Cross told a magazine writer that he'd made the initial discovery, not Harris, with a chunk of gold the size of a hen's egg. But this controversy doesn't matter much other than to fuel the flames of other disputations as to the character of Shorty Harris in future dealings, especially with Pete Aguereberry at Harrisburg. The truth will never be known for certain, but it also didn't make any financial difference to the discovers of the gold. Cross and Harris were full partners in the discovery and shared the original Bullfrog claims.

The partners had found one heck of a bonanza, too. When they had the rock assayed in Goldfield, it far exceeded their expectations; they were thinking it would run about $200 to the ton, but it assayed at $665. It was a rich find, and after Shorty and Cross toured the saloons and let out the word, a rush began that, according to Harris, was "… a real stemwinder. It looked as if the whole population of Goldfield was trying to move at once."

The town of Bullfrog sprung up on the flats below the hills, a tent city that was destined to die young. A little over six miles to the south of the Original Bullfrog discovery the city of Rhyolite came into being, and quickly grew into a metropolis with brick and stone buildings. The skeletons of those buildings stand today in mute testimony to Cross's and Harris's great find, and the tremendous effort made by the people who followed them to develop the Bullfrog strike.

A Visit to Rhyolite & Bullfrog

On the day John Glenn returned to space, Suz and I set out to examine these skeletons, and walk in the footsteps of Rainbow Chasers Harris and Cross. Frankly, Shorty Harris intrigues me; at the time of his Bullfrog strike, he was 47 years old and in the prime of his life, keeping up with much younger men. Years later, well into his '70s, he was still tough enough to wander the desert as a prospector. He wasn't in it for the gold itself; he threw that away every time he found it. It was the life that he loved. He wasn't in it for the possibility of becoming rich. He never had any riches as society might measure them; he was born poor, lived poor, and died poor. But by all accounts he was a happy man. His wealth was in the joy of his life.

Death Valley

Ruins at Rhyolite.

Rhyolite is about six miles west of the town of Beatty. Some active mining still goes on in the area, although the largest of the mines shut down in the winter of 1998. There is still gold in the rock, but the owners are awaiting a rise in the price before reopening the diggings.

Rhyolite still stands. This town was not built to die; its founders planned for it to last. They truly believed Rhyolite would be a center of mining for centuries to come. Their dreams were not to be, however. Several solid but empty old buildings stand in mute testimony to their efforts.

Two trailer camps have sprung up for semi-permanent residents. An art colony is on the southern edge of town. At the colony stand several wood monuments, to the chagrin of the Bureau of Land Management – they want everything here to blend into the desert scenery. These monuments definitely don't blend with anything around here. They are startling caricatures, including a pink lady, a collection of religious icons, and one curious piece: a prospector, swinging a pick, with what appears to be a penguin behind him.

Farther up the road is Rhyolite's famous **bottle house**. Built by Tom Kelly in 1906, it took 50,000 beer bottles to construct it. It's a testament to the thirst of Rhyolite's natives that the two-year-old town could quickly generate that many bottles. The bottle house, like most of the town, is under the protection of the BLM.

A caretaker lives in a travel trailer next to the house. He is there to answer questions and protect the remaining structures. He looks the part. Clint Boehringer, a retiree from Oregon, has been staying as Rhyolite's BLM caretaker ev-

Clint Boehringer, caretaker of the Bottle House.

ery winter, from November to April, for the last seven years. His sun-darkened face is offset by a long gray beard, and flowing gray hair. His suspender-slung jeans are worn and faded, like his cotton shirt.

"I've been come here every winter since 1955," he said. "I had a union job, and we had the Christmas season off. There's no better time to be here. We used to come down the old prospectors' trails. Some of them have been closed off by the BLM now as wilderness territory so you can't travel them any more."

Boehringer's passionate interest is the history of Death Valley, and particularly Rhyolite. One of the attractions he favors is the bottle house. Until the BLM took it over, the house had been in use by several Rhyolite residents.

"Tommy Thompson used to have this place, and he built it up pretty good before he died in '74," he said. "Before that, the house was used in a movie in 1925, and later an old-timer named Louis Murphy and a lady named Bessie Moffat kept it up as a museum till Murphy died in '56."

Boehringer, as befits a local historian, was familiar with the stories about Shorty Harris.

"Did you see the statue of the miner with the penguin behind him?" He asked. "That's a tribute to Shorty. When he'd be out on the desert and would take up drinking from his bottle of O, Be Joyful, after a time he'd look behind him and see a penguin following him around. He didn't see pink elephants, he saw penguins."

Shorty and his penguin.

Following Boehringer's directions, we drove past the site of Bull-frog – now just a mud wall or two, fading back into the desert, blending in approved BLM style – and followed a dirt road toward the original Bullfrog. About 2½ miles from Rhyolite we took the fork to the right, and wheeled along a cut in the hillside till we came to the tailings of a mine.

Climbing out of the Jeep, we stepped on the desert sand that Shorty Harris walked, and examined the bits of quartz and the few odd floats of green rock that remained after nearly a century of mining and prospecting. With Shorty looking over our shoulder, Suz and I wandered downstream, prospecting as we went. He might have had a fit, or he might have liked the electronic prospecting tools we used: a Gold Bug metal detector, a device that was built to find nuggets of gold. It is a much easier tool to use than the pick and shovel. He probably would have had the fit; he took a lot of pride in proclaiming himself a "jackass prospector" and he didn't like the "flivver prospectors" that started coming around when cars become common.

But our stop in the gullies below the Original Bullfrog didn't make us any money, not even as much as Shorty Harris's prospecting benefited him nearly a century ago. But then, O, Be Joyful got the best of Shorty. Not long after his strike he threw a major toot and sold his interest in the discovery claim for $1,000. When he woke up from his drunken spree he found himself to be nothing but a single-blanket-jackass-prospector again, and promptly blew the rest of his money on more O, Be Joyful.

But his partner Cross did very well. He also sold his claim, but for $125,000, and bought a ranch with the proceeds of his Rainbow Chasing. Shorty loaded up his burros and headed for Ballarat.

Ballarat

The town of Ballarat was born to serve the gold miners and prospectors who worked the Panamints during the 1890s. There wasn't much to Ballarat, and its location in the Panamint Valley was less than ideal. Located on the edge of a salt flat, the weather is atrociously hot in summer, as high as 120°, and bitterly cold in winter due to the winds coming off the snow-laden Panamint Mountains.

Ballarat, at the foot of the Panamints.

Even so, the town grew to some 500 residents, and boasted the Calloway Hotel, a dozen saloons, and two stores, but not a single church. It primarily served the laborers at the gold mines that were being developed nearby and the prospectors that roamed the hills. Ballarat served as a supply point and a party town, and stands in history as the town that supplied many a great story about Shorty Harris. One of the best is the story of his first funeral – the one he lived to tell about. Whether it is true or not, who knows? But it certainly should be true.

Shorty Harris's First Funeral

One Fourth of July Ballarat was celebrating, and Shorty was there. The party had gone on for two days, and Shorty was three sheets to the wind. He was a little under the weather, too, from the two-day hooraw. He finally passed out.

His friends had an idea that would wake him up and sober him down, so he could enjoy the rest of the party. They gathered up some boards and threw together a coffin, then gently laid the snoring Shorty to rest. They placed the coffin on a pool table in Chris Wicht's saloon, and the bartender kept an eye on him while he slept the afternoon away.

When Shorty began to stir, the bartender spread the word. Soon votive candles were lit and the Rainbow Chasers gathered around the pool table, speaking softly to each other of Shorty's life. Shorty's eyes opened, but he didn't move, while his friends prayed over him and sang his praises.

Finally the candles were blown out and the boys picked up the coffin for the trek out to the graveyard. Then Shorty started yelling, and word has it that he jumped out of his coffin and ran out the door of Chris Wicht's saloon, not returning to Ballarat for several months when the shock finally wore off.

As towns go, even in its heyday Ballarat never was much of a place; and today it's even less. It's located on the southern end of Panamint Valley, north of Trona. Much of the town is privately owned, and even though it is designated as an Historical Site only its few remaining residents – not the BLM or any other government agency – protect the town from the depredations of unthinking visitors.

The scenery is out of this world.

Right behind the town the Panamint Mountains rise almost straight up off the valley floor, in the space of just a few miles. Across the valley, the mountains that make up the Argus Range seem nearly as tall. The view from Ballarat is stupendous: a long dry lakebed at your feet, desert flats with creosote and the occasional Joshua, the colorful canyon walls of the Panamints and deep blue mountains in the distance, lined with scars and cliffs. It is colorful, wild, rugged, and empty.

Here, Shorty Harris lived out his golden years, in an adobe-mud shanty near Wicht's saloon. From this headquarters he'd head out on prospecting expeditions, nearly always with a partner, and here he kept his old mule. Long after the mule had gone blind he took care of her and let her live out her remaining years happily.

Now in Ballarat there's a small general store, a couple of shanties, and a trailer park area. There's an equipment yard, somewhat hidden from view, that mars the view to the east only for a moment. An old truck – reputed to be one of Charlie Manson's – turns out to be a true antique, a '40s-vintage Dodge Power Wagon.

At the general store, a veranda provides shade from the westering sun. There's a round table, with patio chairs, and two men sitting, one of them sipping a beer. From their table you can look out over the valley, a peaceful sight that never tires the eyes. There's the main road, which seldom has any cars on it; the Argus Mountains, brooding and mysterious; and the desert, unending.

The gent with the beer is wearing Western boots, the old style that goes up to the knee, and a vest over a plain shirt. He introduces himself as "Gangrene Gene" Curry, and the three pistols he's packing are authentic and old. They are black powder pieces that appear to date back to the 1880s.

"I'm the Marshall here," Curry says, "And Lightfoot Louie here is the mayor and the storekeeper."

Louie Shanteler is a young man, perhaps in his early 20s, who grew up in Ridgecrest. He lives here, in the caretaker's trailer across the street, and tends the general store for the owners, who are absentees. They own the junk behind the store as well, an eyesore, we all agree. Curry lives in a trailer in the lot across town – perhaps 300 yards away. Often, these two are the only people in town. Sometimes Shanteler is alone here, when Curry goes down south to earn his wages.

"We get a lot of tourists sometimes, though," Shanteler said, "And you should see it on the weekends. We'll have several people camping here, to go four-wheeling or whatever."

The trailer camp costs $1.50 a night, which is a donation to the Ballarat Restoration Fund.

"We want to rebuild these places, make it exactly like it was," Curry said. He pointed out to me where Chris Wicht's saloon used to be; just the outline remained. Wicht was a popular barkeep and his place was one of the most popular hangouts on the desert. When the town died he closed the bar and stayed in his cabin up the canyon, where, according to Curry, he drank himself to death. "It was the biggest and best saloon in town, heck, in the whole region," he said. "Wicht even had a pool table."

Shorty's mud hut wasn't standing any longer, but one just like it was still up, on the main road coming from the dry lake.

"People think that was Shorty's cabin, because there is a picture of him standing in front of it, but that isn't it," Curry said. "Shorty's was two doors down." I asked the pair about Shorty's reputation, and whether he was a little loose with the truth. "He was a miner," Shanteler said, with a shrug and half a grin.

An old miner's cabin at Ballarat.

Not much remains of the original Ballarat. A couple of mud huts, former miner's homes, and the old assay office are still standing, but the highlight of the trip is the Ballarat graveyard. It's the resting place for more than a dozen souls that met their end in Ballarat. Most famous is "Seldom Seen" Slim, a prospector who came to Ballarat in 1917, lived out his life here and spent most of his time on the desert hunting minerals. He died here in the 1960s. His funeral made the national television news, as he was the last of the old time Rainbow Chasers.

"I got to meet him once," Curry said. "We only talked for five minutes, but I'll never forget it. It was like meeting a legend. He was the last of the old-timers."

Before we leave, Curry has one more thing to tell us, something incongruous with his six-guns and Old West outfit:

"Hey, you get a chance, be sure to go and check out our website. Some guy in town made it for us. I've been told it's real good, but I've never seen it."

Shorty's Second Strike

Shorty Harris hit his big payday more than once. The second time he made the map with a discovery in the Panamints. While out traveling with another prospector, Pete Aguereberry, Shorty not only made his mark with another good claim, he had a town named after him.

The year was 1906. Shorty had recently lost his claim at Bullfrog, and while heading back to the Panamints he ran into Pete, who decided to ride along. Crossing the Panamints was a hard and dangerous business, and nobody wanted to do it alone; travelers would team up for safety and comfort.

Shorty was on his way to Ballarat for (what else?) the big Fourth of July celebration. Aguereberry was going to Ballarat to collect a grubstake and head out to do more prospecting. On a big flat south of what would become Skidoo, the pair found gold. One or the other of them did; they both claimed to have made the discovery.

Pete's story makes the most sense. Pete was a greenhorn with little prospecting experience. Until recently, he'd been tending sheep over in the Central Valley, near Madera, and had come to the desert with a herd to tend. When that job played out he joined the rush to find gold in the Death Valley region. So Pete didn't have the years of experience of knowing where to look for the elusive gold metal.

The flats where they found gold was on the trail between Death Valley and Ballarat, a location that had been traveled over hundreds of times by experienced prospectors, including Shorty. The location was not one that met the usual geological qualifications for gold strikes; it just wasn't the kind of place that Shorty would have bothered to prospect. Pete wasn't experienced enough to know this, however, so he looked – and made a strike.

After a quick trip to Wildrose Canyon for a supply of water, Shorty and Pete staked out claims for themselves and a few friends, then hurried down to Ballarat to spread the news. Pete returned first with a group from Ballarat – history doesn't say where Shorty was, but Wicht's saloon is a good bet. Pete found that some hopeful boys from Wildrose Canyon had already gotten the word, boys like the outlaws who had made it big in Panamint City. They had jumped his claim, pulling out his location notices and replacing them with their own. Pete, backed up by the party from Ballarat, convinced the claim jumpers they were in the wrong, and won back the claims.

A tent city quickly grew, and in days some 300 miners were working the flats. The town was named Harrisberry, named for both of the founders (Shorty *Harris* and Pete Aguere*berry*). Somehow it later transformed to Harrisburg – some blame Shorty for that, but most likely it just happened – and Shorty must have had big hopes for his namesake. Yet, true to form, after a while Shorty sold out his interest in the claim and wandered off.

It soon became apparent that this was a small strike and the tents were struck, bringing an end to Harrisburg. The town was in its last throes when an even bigger deposit was found over the hill in Skidoo. Later, Pete bought back the original Harrisberry claims and worked the mine for the rest of his life, earning a respectable living.

We have one more stop on our trail of Shorty Harris. The other place we have to go is south of Furnace Creek in Death Valley itself.

Here Shorty is buried. He died in Lone Pine in 1934, but as a last request his remains were buried next to his friend Jim Dayton, in the valley they had both come to love. He wrote his own epitaph, and it says it all:

"Bury me beside Jim Dayton in the valley we loved. Above me write: Here lies Shorty Harris, a single-blanket jackass prospector."

Shorty's grave.

If You Go

Beatty *is 115 miles north of Las Vegas on US Highway 95. Full services are available there, including a couple of casinos where visitors can pay those "Nevada taxes" with the slot machines or the card tables.*

Rhyolite *is about six miles west of the town of Beatty on State Route 374.*

Continuing westward on 374 takes you through Death Valley National Park. Get fuel and provisions in Beatty, as they are expensive and scarce in the park.

To find **Harrisburg**, *take the Emigrant Gap Road west of Stovepipe Wells. Check with the rangers at Stovepipe Wells to make sure the road is open. There's nothing left of Harrisburg.*

Ballarat *is in the Panamint Valley, across the dry lakebed from the Trona-Wildrose Road (also the Panamint Valley Road). Turn south from Highway 190 toward Trona. In this area, the nearest services are at the Panamint Springs resort on Highway 190, in Trona, and in Ridgecrest.*

Death Valley

Shorty's grave is located in Death Valley, across the lake from Badwater. To get there, take the Westside Road south of Furnace Creek to the Eagle Borax works (a long dusty trip down a washboarded road). Check with the rangers and get a good map before attempting this trip. This site is in the heart of Death Valley, one of the hottest and most unforgiving places in the world.

The Panamints

The Panamint Mountains encapsulated the dreams and hopes of generations of Rainbow Seekers. Today, they continue to entice gold prospectors and wanderers with promises of riches – whether it is gold or silver or peace they are seeking.

A view of the Panamints from Trona Road.

The Panamints are big, bold, beautiful mountains that rise between Death Valley to the east and a salt flat plain to the west. With Telescope Peak as its centerpiece, the mountains are snow-laden in win-

Above: Dunes & Brush © *William Van Doren*

Below: Window Rock, AZ

Above: Clay Canyon © William Van Doren

Opposite: Hoodoos at Bryce Point

Below: Monument Valley

Above: White Dunes © *William Van Doren*

Opposite: Hoodoos at Bryce Canyon

Below: Mesquite Flat Dunes © *William Van Doren*

Above: Artist's Pallette © William Van Doren

Opposite: Three Sisters formation, Monument Valley

Below: Zabrinski Point © William Van Doren

ter, cool havens in summer and hellaciously steep any time of the year. Rugged and beautiful, the mountains are a panorama of color that show off their geological history in the layered patterns of their sheer rock walls.

And these mountains are rich in Western history too, the birthplace of some of the best campfire tales to come out of the West. One of the best stories has to do with how the first valuable minerals in the Panamints were found.

The First Strike

Back in the early 1870s, the Panamints were a "Robber's Roost" – a place with no law, no civilization, and a haven for outlaws and cutthroats. They were also home to prospectors exploring Death Valley, as the mountains provided relief from the intense heat of summer.

In the fall of 1872, three prospectors – Robert Stewart, William Kennedy, and Richard Jacobs – were hunting in the Panamints for the famous Lost Gunsight mine. They followed one of the southernmost canyons almost to the crest of the range, and discovered an immense outcropping of silver-laden quartz.

By the time they made the strike, it was early December and winter had come hard. Snowstorms covered the Panamints, and the three barely had enough time to collect some silver specimens then head downstream.

Back in civilization, the specimens assayed out to a fortune, and the trio made plans to return to their discovery. Maintaining the secret of their find for the months that the source of the rock remained inaccessible because of winter storms must have been pure hell for them. They spent those months on the slopes of the Panamints, and in early April, they loaded up and headed back up the canyon.

While waiting, however, they'd come to the attention of one of the outlaw gangs in the area. Six bandits – Henry Gibbons, Dan Tipton, James Dempsey, James Bruce, William Cannin, and Louis Hudon – were wanted in Nevada for robbing the Pioche stage. Wells Fargo had put up a reward for the men and they had to hide out until things

Death Valley

Opposite: Devil's Golf Course © *William Van Doren*

cooled off. These were ruthless killers, quite at home in the lawless free-for-all mining camps and owlhoot hangouts where no man with a badge would ever come.

The Gibbons gang somehow got wind of the find and kept an eye on the three prospectors. When they headed up-canyon in April, the gang followed.

Jacobs, who had evolved into the leader of the trio of prospectors, was well aware of the bandits. He knew that things could go sour very quickly for them, as soon as the outlaws became aware of the fortune ahead. The odds were not good for surviving the coming confrontation – six killers with "enough guns to stock a hardware store" against three peaceful prospectors. He realized that their only hope for survival was to share the discovery and let the outlaws stake their own claims. There was enough silver-rich ground for all, but he had to convince them of that.

When the canyon widened and the rich, rich silver quartz lodes on both sides of the canyon came into view, the prospectors and the bandits came together. Gunplay was forgotten as all nine men gazed at the rich vistas, and the size of the bonanza seized their minds. All nine scrambled up the slopes and began staking claims – ironically, what would be the richest claim of all was the one the badman Gibbons filed. The bandit made the best payday of his life without firing a shot.

Finding a bonanza is one thing, but making it pay is quite another. So far from civilization, with no roads, no ready supply of materials or labor, made development of the mining operations extremely costly and risky. It takes capital, lots of capital, to dig the mineral from the earth and convert it to cash, resting safely in a bank.

Thus enter Nevada's Silver Senators onto the scene at Panamint.

The Silver Senators – John P. Jones and William Stewart – had made their fortunes in the Washoe country, Stewart by litigating claims and Jones by mining. Stewart was a lawyer who had helped write Nevada's constitution. Together they were a formidable team and they were well known in mining circles, with the cash and resources needed to develop a huge new field.

They purchased all of the new Panamint claims – and arranged for Wells Fargo to drop the charges on the Gibbons gang by allowing the robbers to pay back the money they'd stolen. The purchase price was over a quarter-million dollars, a sum that made headlines in mining camps all around the region and touched off a new rush to the Panamints. If the Senators were willing to sink this much into bare ground, then fortunes must be waiting to be made.

Panamint City

So this was the birth of Panamint City, a shantytown built in a canyon so narrow that there was room only for one street. It was remote and wild, a place far from law and order and existing only as long as the silver did.

The outlaws' mine was one of several that were being developed in Surprise Canyon. It took money to develop the rich outcroppings of silver – big money. The interest of the Comstock mine developers was enough to spark a rush of not only Rainbow Seekers to the area, but big-money investors who bought into the companies that were formed. The Silver Senators provided the startup funds, but development money came in the form of stock sales in the major financial circles of San Francisco and New York. These stock promotions fanned the flames of Panamint and the rush was on.

As Panamint's tent city and clapboard shacks grew, mining went on at a hectic pace. The mines were so close to the city, which was built in Surprise Canyon itself, that sometimes the charges of dynamite would blow rocks and dirt onto the mules and wagons parked on the street.

It was a wild and woolly town, with no law and few amenities. Houses and stores rose from the canyon walls, built of stone or piñon, and later of boards hauled in from forests far away. The town had six general stores, selling eggs for $2 a dozen; the Bank of Panamint City; a dozen or more saloons; and a newspaper, which became well known for its feisty attitude, the *Panamint News*. By 1874, seven stages a week brought newcomers to the city. Miners and gamblers, whores and preachers lived in shanties built on the sides of the canyon, off trails that were too steep for horses or mules.

Death Valley

The ore from the outlaws' mines was incredibly rich, but still needed smelting and transporting. These were big-ticket expenses, due to Panamint's remote location. Jones became the "money man" – working back East and in the coastal cities, raising money for development and planning a new railroad. Stewart was the man on site, in charge of developing the mines and getting the silver to market.

Reducing the ore to silver as close to the mine as possible made sense as it cut the cost of shipping. So in 1875 the Senators financed a stamp mill and a smelter. As the mines continued to spew silver-rich rock, the smelter reduced it to bullion and Senator Stewart arranged for his first shipment.

Outsmarting the Outlaws

But shipping the silver out was a big problem. There was 200 miles of desert to cross, and the Panamints were still an outlaw haven. There was no law, and the robber's roost in Wildrose Canyon was still home to the worst elements in the country. Panamint City itself was no place for the faint of heart. The reputation of the area was so bad that not even Wells Fargo, who seldom let bank robbers and thieves keep them from making money, would open an express office. They refused to handle the silver shipments.

A pair of two-bit outlaws made their home in a canyon on the western slope of the Panamints. These two – John Small and John McDonald – were a pair of hard-luck bumbling criminals, whose most famous robbery was of a Wells Fargo stage that netted them $18. It also put them on wanted posters, and drove them to their hideout in Wildrose Canyon. As the Silver Senator built his smelter, these two outlaws made their brags around town that the first shipment would be theirs.

The big day came, and the outlaws entered the mine office with six-guns drawn. Senator Stewart calmly invited them to have at the silver, to steal what they could. But they could not do much, as the Senator's smelter, instead of melting the silver into bars, had made huge, 400-pound squares of silver.

The boys tried to heft the silver bars onto the back of a mule, but could not begin to lift them. The mule protested being used in such a fashion and would have nothing to do with the enterprise; bucking and kicking, it ran away from the men, who realized they were beaten by the 400-pound ingenuity of the Senator.

The bad boys of Panamint City rode out of town empty-handed, stumped and defeated by the wily man of the Comstock. The 400-pound bars of silver were safely transported for months out Panamint City, without even an armed guard, on wagons provided by desert freight-master Remi Nadeau. They crossed 200 miles of desert, every bit as safe in the wagon as they would be in a Wells Fargo safe. No one could lift them out – or cash them in if they did steal them.

It was more than the outlaw pair could endure. After a few months of watching the wagons roll safely to Los Angeles, without the Senator paying even the slightest courtesy and respect by providing an armed guard, the pair gave up any plans to steal the silver. They robbed Panamint City's general store and rode away forever.

The rest of Panamint City wasn't long in following the outlaws down the canyon. The silver strike played out about a year later. Mine after mine closed down after reaching the end of the paydirt. In the spring of 1876 the Silver Senators closed their mill, but the miners kept digging and exploring for more silver-bearing ore. But the heyday was done, and by May of 1877 the last mines closed and Panamint City was a ghost town.

If You Go

The eastern slope of the Panamints forms the westward wall of Death Valley. The western slope, where you'll find Wildrose Canyon, Harrisburg Flats, Ballarat, and Panamint City, is accessed three ways.

From Death Valley: On Highway 190, east of Stovepipe Wells, a road takes off through Emigrant Canyon to near Skidoo, Wildrose Canyon, Harrisburg, and Aguereberry Point. This road was closed as a result of flood damage that occurred during the El Niño storms of 1998. The road joins the main highway to Trona and Ridgecrest.

Death Valley

The Emigrant Canyon Road can be bypassed by continuing on Highway 190 through Towne's Pass. You'll drop into the Panamint Valley, cross the dry Panamint lake, then turn south at the intersection with the Trona-Wildrose Road, which becomes Highway 178 in Trona and leads you on to Ridgecrest.

From the west: From Highway 395 – the major north-south route from the Los Angeles area to Bishop and points north – take Highway 190 east from Olancha. You'll pass by Dirty Socks Spring on the southern edge of Owens Lake, then cut southeast through the Darwin Hills. The road touches the beautiful Rainbow Canyon, then brings you to Panamint Springs and the Trona-Wildrose Road.

From the south: From Ridgecrest, head east on State Highway 178 past the Trona Pinnacles, through Trona. You'll cross over a small pass and drop into Panamint Valley near Ballarat on the Trona-Wildrose Road.

Services: *Except for the small general store in Ballarat, which may or may not be open, the only services available in the whole valley are at Panamint Springs, which is a very nice resort. Stock up and gas up at Olancha, Trona, Ridgecrest, or Stovepipe Wells.*

Ridgecrest is the nearest major city with a good selection of services. There are many motels, restaurants, garages, and gas stations there. Trona is a small mining town with a few motels and cafés.

Don't go here without adequate emergency supplies – the Trona-Wildrose Road is very lonely and this is a vast desert.

Highlights

◈ **Ballarat:** On the south end of the valley, a dirt road takes off to the east, past a radar station to the town of Ballarat. There's camping and a small general store there. At the turnoff from the Trona-Wildrose Road, there's a sign and a historical marker.

◈ **Panamint City:** This is up Surprise Canyon above Ballarat. It is a difficult four-wheel-drive trip, and a winch is required. I never made it up there.

◈ **Trona Pinnacles:** These weird Tufa rock formations are south of Panamint Valley between Trona and Ridgecrest, and are worth the trip if you are anywhere near. If you're a science fiction fan you might recognize these formations; they've been used by Hollywood to portray other worlds.

The Trona Pinnacles rising from the surrounding land.

◈ **Wildrose Canyon:** Here is the home of outlaws and charcoal kilns. If the access through Emigrant Canyon is closed from Stovepipe Wells, the road from Panamint should be open.

◈ **Harrisburg, Aguereberry Point, and Skidoo:** These famous places are beyond Wildrose Canyon. Aguereberry Point is one of the most beautiful lookouts anywhere in America. From high in the Panamints –

over 6,000 feet – you look down into Death Valley to the east, and clear to the Sierras in the west. The road to the lookout was built by Pete Aguereberry. He just wanted to share the beautiful scenery with anyone willing to make the trip; he never charged anyone, or accepted a fee, for using his road to the lookout point that now bears his name. The road goes by his mine and home on Harrisburg Flat.

Harrisburg, which wasn't ever much more than a tent city, is completely gone. Skidoo has vanished also. Only a few mines remain.

Up this canyon are three Death Valley National Park campgrounds that are open in the summer only and, according to the Park Service, can be accessed only with a four-wheel-drive vehicle.

◈ **Navy jets:** You'll have no choice here; they like to buzz through the Panamint Valley at high speed and low altitude. It's a bit startling to be traveling along an empty desert trail and have your bones rattled by the roar of a jet fighter.

Death Valley Scotty

We have to talk about Death Valley Scotty. I don't want to; he was a fraud and a charlatan and not worthy of this magnificent place. But I don't have a choice. What is particularly galling is that's just the way Scotty planned it. People had to talk about him then, and we have to talk about him now.

Scotty's name permanently resides on a mansion that a Chicago millionaire built in the northern end of the valley. The millionaire, one Albert Johnson, was a heavy investor in Death Valley Scotty, and he paid for constructing the mansion but let Scotty claim ownership of it. The old Grapevine Ranch headquarters will always be Scotty's Castle, and the story of it will tell the story of their times.

Scotty's Castle is an incredible piece of work, located in the middle of desert, miles from any town. A huge Spanish-style villa, it houses a fine art collection, museum pieces, and treasures from around the world. It is now owned by the National Park Service and is used as a public museum.

Scotty's Castle.

Scotty – Walter Scott to his parents – was born September 20, 1872, in Kentucky, the son of a horse breeder who made whiskey on the side. The youngest of six children, his mother died while he was still a baby, and he grew up feeling unwanted and alone. He ran away from home when he was 14 to join his brothers who were working as cowboys in Wells, Nevada. Scotty had flair with the horses and became a skilled rider, often starring in local rodeos. In the 1890s he rode in Buffalo Bill Cody's Wild West Show. He loved the stage, and quickly learned how to huckster with the best.

After leaving that job – apparently his last honest employment – Scotty did what many men did on the desert; he found businessmen to grubstake him while he searched for gold. Only thing is, he did it many times, selling more than 100% of what he might find, and he sold pieces of mines that never existed. He also didn't spend much time out prospecting; he was too busy mining the pocketbooks of the people who trusted him.

Death Valley

That in itself wasn't too unusual for the times; some people were very free with the truth and in those days, stock frauds were common, as were prospectors who spent more time collecting grubstakes than prospecting. But Scotty had a real gift for showmanship, a crafty mind, a desire for wealth without effort, and a craving for publicity. His golden tongue created a reputation for him that made real rainbow-chasin' prospectors laugh in derision, but caught the attention of newspapermen and the public. This, coupled with the stock frauds being perpetrated in the area, made a ripe combination. It was a mining stock fraud that propelled Scotty into national headlines.

Prospectors were just the first step in mining. Seldom would a prospector actually mine for the metals he'd found. He'd usually sell his prospect to a developer, who would have the cash and the resources to fully assess the find and begin converting the raw material into wealth. It took money – big money – to make a mine pay. There was equipment to buy, buildings to put up, and men to hire; all this took capital.

So the developer would form a company and print up shares. He'd sell these on the stock market, in towns like San Francisco or New York, to generate millions of dollars of development capital. With this much money in the offing, and the few controls and regulations on the markets in those days, it isn't surprising that many, many of the stock offerings never paid off – and some of them were outright frauds.

By 1905, the bloom was off the rose in Death Valley mining stocks; so many investors had been burned that they were getting a little wiser to the tricks of the con men. But some easy money was still out there, if a good huckster knew how to work his mark.

"Mysterious Scott," as he was known then, had the flair and the skill to work the crowd. He pulled a small fortune out of easterners, most notably Julius Gerard, the third vice president of the Knickerbocker Trust Company, and Albert Johnson, an insurance executive in Chicago. These two men, and some others to a lesser extent, financed Scotty's prospecting trips.

Eventually, Gerard realized he'd been conned, and took it hard; he sued Scotty, but collected only a dozen worthless claims. Johnson took the knowledge that Scotty was a charlatan rather well. They became lifelong friends. But before this, Scotty had become a household name, thanks to his talent for self-promotion and the desperate straits one Death Valley mining developer and stock promoter had found himself in.

E. Burdon Gaylord had bought an option on a prospect near the Keane Wonder, the Big Bell, with $25,000 down and the balance due in a year. His plan was to sell his option at a big profit before the year was out. But Shorty Harris had, unintentionally, done him in, by finding the bigger strike at Bullfrog. Interest in the Keane Wonder area had fallen off and the "smart money" was going to Rhyolite and Bullfrog.

At this point, Death Valley Scotty enters the stage.

According to Lingenfelter in his book *Death Valley and the Amargosa*, Gaylord was desperate, and he saw Death Valley Scotty as a magnificent conman. He figured he could use Scotty's antics – which even then were making headlines in the California press – as a way to drum up excitement about Death Valley mining properties, which would give him a chance to unload his option at a profit, or at least recoup his investment.

So Gaylord allegedly bankrolled Scotty and sent him to Los Angeles, where he made quite a stir. The newspapers ate it up, celebrating the "Death Valley Croesus" who had come to town and spent $2,600 in three days seeing the sites. He would work at being mysterious. He would appear in town at odd intervals, spend money like it was water, then he'd disappear, back to the desert. He'd drop hints about his gold mine in the desert, and tell all about the riches in Death Valley.

All this played well with the Los Angeles papers, but that wasn't good enough for Gaylord. He wanted New York money to take the Big Bell off his hands. So Scotty came up with a scheme that placed him on the front pages of papers across the country: he'd rent a train to make a record-breaking run from Los Angeles to Chicago. For $5,500, the Santa Fe railroad set him up with a special train, the "Death Valley Coyote," guaranteed to make it to Chicago within 48 hours. On July 9, 1905, the train left Los Angeles with a crowd of

1,500 in attendance – and it was in Chicago 45 hours later, to the cheers of thousands at the stations it passed through.

This stunt made Death Valley Scotty. He was famous now, and his strange promotion worked: interest in Death Valley mining was at an all-time high. Investors were easy to find now, and Scott had no trouble getting more grubstakes and selling off pieces of his nonexistent gold mine. But Gaylord wasn't able to cash in on the game he'd set up. He had to forfeit his option in the Big Bell.

The strange story of Mysterious Scott has many more chapters. His charades and shenanigans kept him in the press, and the profligate spending convinced his backers that there was indeed a gold mine – though some of them finally began to suspect that the gold mine wasn't a hole in the ground, it was the hole in their pockets.

His biggest backer – Albert Johnson, who had put up more than $20,000 at this point in the Scott parade – gradually began to realize that there was no gold mine, and that he'd been pick-pocketed by one of the best con men to come out of the West. As the years passed this realization grew. Scotty was eventually exposed and even confessed to his massive frauds. But this did not end the strange association between Johnson and Scott; in fact, it strengthened it.

Johnson had been crippled in a train wreck at an early age. His life was one of pain, which was eased on his trips to Death Valley with Scott. He came to love the desert land and forgave Scotty his aberrations. Eventually, with his wife, he moved to Death Valley and built the Castle at a spot chosen by Scotty. He shared the Castle with Scotty, and continued to finance his antics – strictly for laughs, he said in later years.

So that's the story of the strange castle out in the middle of nowhere, up in Grapevine Canyon, built by a multimillionaire for a man who conned him out of thousands and thousands of dollars, but became a friend.

Scotty's Castle *(as it's known, even if Albert Johnson built it) is in Grapevine Canyon about 40 miles north of the Furnace Creek-Stovepipe Wells area in the heart of Death Valley. There's a good road to the Castle from the central area of the Park. It can also be reached from Highway 95 in Nevada.*

The Castle is actually outside of Death Valley, a short ways up the canyon. Tours of the mansion, which is filled with antiques and artifacts from the early 20th century, are offered daily for a nominal fee. The last tour of the day begins at 4:30.

Joshua Tree National Park

W ild rock formations, beautiful Joshua forests, oases with tall, stately palm trees – Joshua Tree National Park forms the southern border of the Mojave and is a popular recreation area. Here, the Mojave and the Sonoran/Colorado Deserts meet. In the transition zone, representatives of both deserts thrive.

Joshua Tree became a National Monument in 1936, and a National Park in 1994. It's huge: 60 miles east to west, 30 miles north to south. The rock formations are world-famous among climbers, who spend months in the park honing their skills. But long before the Park was established as a recreation center for climbers and tourists, or even before the land became a National Monument, Joshua Tree was the home of some unusual Rainbow Chasers and desert rats who own the right to a share of history. One of the most interesting of these is a man by the name of Bill Keys.

The Story of Bill Keys

Keys was a rancher and miner with a fascinating skill for improvising something out of nothing. His Desert Queen ranch still stands as a monument to man who could make do – and do very well – far from town, with his wits as his primary tool; he was a real American pioneer. He also was a man who was not afraid to fight. He had three shooting incidents. Two of the shootouts put him in jail for a short time and one landed him in prison. Both of these incidents occurred, not in the 1800s but in the 1900s – the third in 1943.

Keys was born on Sept. 27, 1879, in Russia. He was George Barth then, the son of German-born parents who immigrated to the United States. They lived in Kansas, but the future Bill Keys left home at the age of 15, wandering through the Southwestern states. In Arizona he was recruited to join Teddy Roosevelt's Rough Riders. When he enlisted he took his new name (William Key; he later added the "s"), but serious illness kept him from serving. He was discharged from the hospital and the Rough Riders and wandered farther west, spending a year as a deputy sheriff in Kingman, Arizona, then set out prospecting in Death Valley and the Mojave. He spent time in Goldfield, Rhyolite, Randsburg, and Searchlight; his wanderings took him to the hot spots and he prospected the barren hills with the likes of Shorty Harris – and Mysterious Scott, better known by this time as Death Valley Scotty. He became involved in one of Scotty's more notorious escapades and ended up in jail for it.

Scotty was scheming to sell another nonexistent mine to some Eastern investors. He hired Keys and another cowboy to scare them off by shooting over their heads in Wingate Pass. The other cowboy was drunk and shot Scotty's brother by mistake. Keys, Scotty, and the cowboy spent time in jail, but were never prosecuted as the investors went back East before the trial was held. Keys, however, later succeeded in finding several legitimate good claims and sold them off to a group of investors.

In 1911, Keys wandered down to what would become Joshua Tree, and there he settled for life. He operated the Tully Mine for a while, and worked for wages at the Desert Queen Mine. But the Desert Queen had been pretty much worked out, and the existing owner could not pay Keys his wages – so he gave him the mine. This began the era of Bill Keys, desert rancher and mine operator – an era that didn't end until his death in 1969.

Keys, now settled as a property owner, loved the desert, and his Desert Queen Ranch. He homesteaded a fine site with water, and began constructing an irrigation system so he could grow fruits and vegetables. He married Frances May Lawton in 1918, and together they built a desert paradise based on hard work and adapting to the land. He raised cattle – which brought him trouble with the big cattle companies, starting with the Barker and Shay Cattle Company, who were pushed off the range near the Desert Queen when Keys homesteaded the watering hole. (That led to his second gunfight, a dispute with a cowboy for the Barker and Shay Company. The cowboy was wounded.)

From 1918 to 1943 the Keys family grew, as did the Desert Queen Ranch. Keys built a schoolhouse and hired a teacher for his kids; later, neighbors moved onto the high desert and their children went to school at the Desert Queen. The district provided a teacher. The family was self-sufficient, with the cattle, their gardens, orchards, gold mining and milling operations. But in 1943 a former deputy from Los Angeles, who apparently was suffering from a brain tumor and delusions about William Keys, shattered their peace and tried to put an end to their desert life.

In 1939, Worth Bagley had medically retired from the Los Angeles County Sheriff's office and purchased an old homestead near the Desert Queen. On his ranch was a road that Keys used regularly to service a well on his ranch, and Bagley resented Keys' use of that road. After several arguments, that resentment boiled over and Bagley ambushed Bill Keys as he drove down the road on May 11, 1943. Bagley got the first shot off, but Keys was a better aim. He killed Bagley, firing three shots in rapid succession with his hunting rifle.

The resulting trial was, to some, a miscarriage of justice. Keys was convicted of manslaughter, primarily because the coroner testified that Bagley had been shot in the back. Other evidence about the dispute between Bagley and Keys, and actions by Keys to resolve the dispute peacefully with local law enforcement, was misrepresented to the jury. Information regarding Bagley's medical condition and evidence about his aberrant behavior was not allowed. Whether the trial errors were caused by the influence of Keys' past association with Scotty and his violent background, machinations of the big cattle companies, or the National Park Service's desire to put an end to Keys' cattle operation, is a hot point of contention and speculation still.

The end result was that Keys went to San Quentin, sentenced to 10 years. He was a model prisoner who spent his time educating himself with books and activities; he referred to this time as his "college." He stubbornly refused to ask for parole, even though he was a candidate for early release, because he did not want to admit guilt or acknowledge that the sentence was just.

He was paroled, however, because of another desert-lover. Author and lawyer Earl Stanley Gardner took on the case with his magazine series *Court of Last Resort*. In this series, Gardner and a group of attorneys investigated cases that appeared to be miscarriages of justice. They presented the evidence in the magazine, then the readers would vote whether or not to pursue a full pardon.

The readers agreed with Keys: he was innocent and should not be in prison. Gardner and his group of investigators continued to seek new evidence, and eventually presented their information to the Governor of California, Earl Warren. Keys was offered an immediate parole – which Gardner convinced him to accept – and eventually received a full pardon. After nearly five years in San Quentin, the quintessential desert rat returned to Joshua Tree to live out his life on the ranch he loved. He died there 20 years later, in 1969.

Now, the Desert Queen Ranch is a National Park Service monument to the frontier spirit and tremendous ingenuity that men like William Keys and women like Frances May Lawton, his wife, had to employ not only to survive, but to flourish in a harsh land.

This is a harsher desert than Lanfair Valley in the Mojave National Preserve, where settlers tried but failed to make the desert grow; and it is much harsher than the Antelope Valley, where carrot farms and suburban home tracts have taken down much of the Joshua and creosote. The rocky, hot terrain now preserved as Joshua Tree National Park is the transition between the high Mojave and the low Colorado desert, and was created to help preserve what was once a threatened species – the glorious Joshua tree.

The Joshua Tree

The Joshua – *Yucca brevifolia* – isn't really a tree, or even a cactus, but a member of the lily family. It was named by early Mormon settlers who fancied that the tree looked like Joshua, with his arms upraised as he led the Israelites into the promised land. Explorer John Fremont didn't think much of it; he said it was "the most repulsive tree in the vegetable kingdom." For all its ugly ruggedness, the Joshua is very particular about where and how it will live; elevation, soil conditions, temperature, water (amount and timing), and the concurrent existence of a particular insect all affect whether the tree can thrive and propagate.

Joshuas won't spread naturally below 3,000 feet. Too much sand and the water won't drain right; too little and the seeds won't take root. The seeds must fall in another bush that allows the young tree to grow, yet protects it – the delicate seedling is tender and makes good eating; it needs to be protected from hungry animals. The plants grow very slowly and its protective spiky leaves don't emerge for two or three years. In the early spring, creamy white blossoms begin to grow on the ends of the Joshua's branches. The blooms last for several months, into early summer, and are very beautiful; but they will not germinate unless the pronuba moth helps it along. The pronuba makes a nest in the blossoms and spreads pollen. It is a mutually beneficial relationship, as the moth gets a home for its young, and the Joshuas get germinated. The Joshua could not propagate without the moth; no other insect can perform this service.

When conditions are right a Joshua will live to a ripe old age. They don't grow rings, so there's no simple way to date them, but the oldest are thought to be between 600 and 1,000 years old. Once the seedling is established in the proper environment, the tree should live a long time; it has few natural enemies. The living wood is too hard even for

Death Valley

woodpeckers, and the spike-like leaves are very effective armor against being chewed by the desert's herbivores. However, the Joshua's worst enemy arrived on the desert scene about a century ago and he has done considerable damage.

As the turn of the 20th century brought more and more people to the desert, Joshuas were ripped out to make room for gardens, farms, houses, and roads, to the point they have nearly disappeared in the Antelope Valley north of Los Angeles. An enterprising printer used Joshua trees to make paper, but fortunately was not successful in marketing his product profitably. As cars became more common, people from the cities made more trips to the desert, and they dug up the unique desert vegetation for transplanting back home. These acts led a southern California woman, Minerva Hoyt of Pasadena, to work for a federal mandate to preserve what is now Joshua Tree National Park. Her efforts convinced President Roosevelt, and he created Joshua Tree National Monument in August of 1936.

≫————————————————————≪

If You Go

Joshua Tree National Park, is east of Los Angeles, north of Interstate 10. There are three main roads into the park: two off Highway 63 near Yucca Valley and Twentynine Palms, and the third east of Indio off Interstate 10.

*Two visitor centers are open to serve the public, and are good places to start your tour of Joshua Tree. The **Oasis Visitor Center** is near Twentynine Palms. The **Cottonwood Center** is located off the I-10 entrance to the park.*

There is a $10 fee per vehicle to enter the park. The fee is good for a week.

*There are many nature trails, hiking trails, and rock climbing areas. The **Geology Tour Road** is a scenic treat, and very educational. The **Desert Queen Ranch** is open only when a tour guide is present.*

No motels or restaurants are within the park. All services are available in Indio, Twentynine Palms, or Yucca Valley.

Campgrounds: Black Rock Canyon *(100 sites);* **Cottonwood** *(62 sites);* **Hidden Valley** *(39 sites);* **Indian Cove** *(107 sites);* **Jumbo Rocks** *(125 sites);* **White Tank** *(15 sites);* **Belle** *(17 sites);* **Ryan** *(29 sites).*

Water *is available only at Black Rock Canyon and Cottonwood. There are no hookups at any of the facilities.*

Bring your own **firewood** *– collecting wood inside the park is prohibited. Some of the campgrounds may be closed in summer.*

Call Joshua Tree National Park, ☎ *760-367-5500, for more information. Or you can call* ☎ *800-365-2267 to reserve campsites in any of the national parks.*

Death Valley

The Colorado Desert

Introduction

O nce the bottom of a sea, the Colorado Desert is the work of a raging Red Bull, as the Colorado River was once known. As the river carved the Grand Canyon and its chasms upstream it deposited the silt here, forming an immense delta – thousands of square miles, as much as two miles deep, covering much of southern California and part of northwestern Mexico – and it filled the Salton Sink.

The California segment of the Sonoran Desert is known as the Colorado Desert because it was created by the raging Red Bull. The Sonoran Desert is 120,000 square miles of low country, covering the land of Baja California and Sonora, Mexico, as well as southwestern Arizona and southeastern California.

Dropping down from Joshua Tree on the highway to Indio, the differences between the Mojave and the Colorado Sonoran Desert slowly reveal themselves. The grass becomes sparse, the creosote bushes smaller and more spread apart; more varieties of cacti appear, and the soil becomes lighter, appearing more burned by the sun. The flora changes in other ways, surprising ways. There are trees on this desert – thin, almost leafless smoke trees, desert acacias, and palo verde. Hidden in the canyons of California, fan palms create an oasis wherever groundwater rises to the surface, and a strange anomaly called an elephant tree lives in the extreme south at locations where it never freezes.

Picking up the freeway and heading westward toward Los Angeles, other changes appear almost by magic – traffic, cities, highways, green acres, and a huge lake, which was created by accident back in 1905. But 1905 wasn't the first time the mighty Colorado drained its waters in the Salton Sink. Several times in its history it has formed a lake even bigger than the present Salton Sea.

One prominent difference between the Sonoran and Mojave is the altitude. Lower elevation means more heat, and a different variety of plants. The Sonoran Desert is drier, and plants need more protection from the heat. Water – in the form of rainfall – is very rare here. This land, more than any other, has been changed by water: first by far too much, then by far too little.

In the last century, water has once again transformed a large part of this desert. This water was not delivered by nature but by the hand of man through irrigation channels. In the Sink from Palm Springs to Calexico, and along the river from Yuma to Needles, crops now grow where there was once just sand. A complex system of irrigation canals, first constructed in the late 1800s, now brings Colorado River water to the Coachella and Imperial Valleys, transforming them into agricultural meccas. And recreational use of this water brings thousands of people to this land each winter. That's the second prominent difference between the Mojave and the Colorado – the southern desert is much more populated, and much more heavily used for both agriculture and recreation.

It's hard to imagine what the first Europeans would think if they were to see this land now. When they came, this was a desert so fearful, so hot, dry and overwhelming that it isolated the coastal settlements from the rest of their empire.

Juan Bautista de Anza's Passage Across the Desert

The first European to spend much time on the Colorado Desert was the Spanish explorer Juan Bautista de Anza. De Anza was looking for a way across the desert to end the isolation of coastal California. His first trip, in 1774, was successful; he established that a determined group could travel overland between the missions along the coast and central Mexico. Explorers had been seeking such a route for almost two centuries.

But the way wasn't easy. From the Tubac mission near present-day Tucson, he led his band of about 35 men westward across southern Arizona, a scorched, empty land, and made friends with the Yuma Indians. He crossed the Colorado – not an easy task in those days; the Red Bull was a wilder, stronger river then – and wandered southward down to the Sea of Cortez, before heading north to what is now called Harper's Well, where he spent some time in the Borrego Springs area. He eventually made it through to the missions.

One year later, in 1775, he returned with some 245 settlers, including women and children, who would create a settlement later to be known as San Francisco. This settlement, which doubled the Spanish population in California, secured California from the Russians, who were attempting to establish a foothold on the northern coast.

It was a remarkable journey. Even though the men, women and children (38 families, plus soldiers, priests and livestock) were crossing 1,800 miles of one of the hottest and driest deserts in the world, only one person – a woman in childbirth – died on the trip. Three children were born on the way. Also, De Anza and his settlers were good ambassadors for the Spanish Empire. De Anza, like Garces and a few others in Spanish America, deplored the way the native Americans were coerced into slavery at some missions. He worked to establish good relations with the Yuma and Cahuilla natives instead of subjugating them.

Near present-day Yuma, the Spanish established an outpost to protect the trail to California. But de Anza's work to treat the Indians with dignity did not last. The Indians who became friends with de Anza did not take well to the men who followed him, who had more traditional attitudes toward natives. The Quechan (Yuma) Indians rose up and massacred them, effectively ending any Spanish hopes of occupation in the Colorado Desert and closing the Sonoran Desert Trail to the California missions.

To honor this outstanding leader and explorer, Congress created the Juan Bautista de Anza National Historic Trail in 1990 to record the overland route of the colonists. The trail runs from Tubac, Arizona,

Colorado Desert

to San Francisco. In the Colorado Desert much of the trail is now a paved highway, but portions of the trail in the Anza-Borrego State Park can be hiked.

It was many years after the Quechan uprising that the Americans came, in the form of mountain men, prospectors and settlers who would begin the process of taming the Colorado for farming and mining.

Anza-Borrego & Pegleg Smith

The western edge of the Colorado Desert has a marvelous pre-serve: Anza-Borrego State Park. It's only 80 miles from the coast, but Anza-Borrego is a world apart. Against a backdrop of high peaks in the coastal range, this is one of the finest places there is to learn about the desert. As Lynne Foster says in her book *Adventuring in the California Desert*, "There is so much to see and do at Anza-Borrego that it defies description; you'll just have to go and see it for yourself."

Anza-Borrego State Park covers a lot of ground, from below sea level to an elevation over 8,000 feet. It extends over more than 600,000 acres, and is one of the most diverse desert landscapes in existence. With over 500 miles of dirt trails – mostly trails on which four-wheel-drive is recommended – the park is an experience for newcomers and long-term desert rats alike. Guided and self-guided nature tours, lectures by knowledgeable rangers, and a wonderful visitor's center filled with resource materials and displays, all make Anza-Borrego a great stop.

The area has a strong Native heritage. Archeologists have found evidence of human occupation in the region as much as 6,000 years ago. When de Anza came through, the land was home to the Kumeyaay tribe, a subgroup of the Yumas, and the Cahuilla tribe, a subgroup of the Shoshone. Both tribes were semi-nomadic. They wintered in the desert lowlands and moved to the higher ground from spring through the acorn and pine nut harvest in the fall. Here in the state park, you'll see their marks on the land. On bedrock outcroppings visitors find where the Natives ground mesquite beans, agave, pine nuts and grass seeds into meal. Often, near where agave still grows, there's a good chance you'll see the remains of a roasting pit, an area of darkened soil approximately 12 feet in diameter, filled with charcoal and fire-broken rock.

Writing this, my mind's eye wanders to the Borrego Valley, with the town of Borrego Springs nestled next to the snowcapped alpine coastal mountains, and I can't go on. I have to agree with Lynne Foster. You must go see it yourself; it defies written explanation.

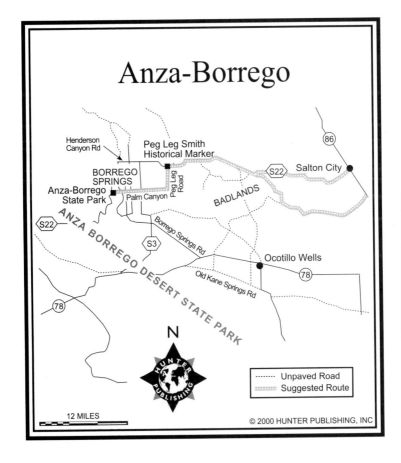

Colorado Desert

While you're there, stop by the Pegleg Smith Monument east of Borrego Springs. Bring 10 rocks to put on the monument (more about that later). It's not likely you'll be the one to find his gold (it's already been found, apparently), but maybe you'll find something else. At any rate, it's a salute to a couple of desert legends who add some of the character of this wonderful land.

The Legend of Pegleg Smith

The desert has always attracted some oddball characters. The legend of Pegleg Smith involves at least three of them and spans two centuries. Actually, it may involve more people; several claiming the name Pegleg Smith have come out of the Colorado Desert. The first, and the one the most credited with the assortment of legends associated with the name, was born Thomas Smith in Garrard County, Kentucky, in 1801. He died near San Francisco in 1866. In the years between, he built a solid reputation as the biggest horse thief, liar, and crook to ever come out of the mountains and bring his talents to California.

Pegleg Smith monument.

In 1827, he was trapping in the Rocky Mountains when Indians wounded him in his left leg, which had to be amputated. He used a wooden leg thereafter, an element that would help Harry Oliver, a well-loved publisher/editor, to build a legend around Pegleg.

Pegleg began his California horse-thieving career in 1829 by stealing 300 horses in the Los Angeles area and herding them to Taos, New Mexico. Rustling became his occupation, at which he achieved the pinnacle of success by helping to steal 3,000 horses in 1839.

While he was exceptionally talented as a horse thief, it is for gold that Smith is best remembered.

The legend is that while he was crossing the Colorado Desert with a partner somewhere near the Salton Sink – probably close to Anza-Borrego – he climbed one of three flat buttes to get his bearings. While there he picked up some unusually heavy black rocks that he assumed to be copper. He put them in his pocket and, much later at a bar in Los Angeles, he discovered that the rocks were gold, covered with a black desert varnish.

He never found the mountain again. He tried, several times. So did others. He told whopping stories about it – and other things – to maintain the legend and his social standing as a liar.

Enter two other desert characters on the scene, long after Pegleg went to his final reward.

The first is **Harry Oliver**, "the old mirage salesman." Oliver was a newspaperman and desert rat who took 35 years off from newspaper publishing and became an award-winning art director in Hollywood. He was a prankster and a character. In 1916 he helped start the Pegleg Smith Club, a group whose aim was to tell the tallest tale. His articles about Pegleg in his *Desert Rat Scrapbook* built upon the legend of the lost gold. To keep people interested, in the 1920s he made a number of wooden peg legs that he aged, then hid out on the desert. Whenever one was found, a new wave of Pegleg gold fever would hit and treasure hunters would load up and head out in search of the black nuggets.

To add further fuel to the flames, Oliver created a monument to Pegleg east of Borrego Springs. He roped off an area and put a sign advising anyone who seeks the gold to add 10 stones to the monument. Then, in 1948, he and others created the Pegleg Smith Liar's Contest, held the first Saturday in April at the monument. The contest is still ongoing.

In 1965, an anonymous reader of *Desert Magazine* reported that he'd found Pegleg's gold, and he wasn't sharing it. He said he had removed over $300,000 worth of nuggets (back when gold was worth $35 an ounce).

According to Choral Pepper, editor of the magazine at that time, she received a package containing two cobbles of peculiar shape – one black as a chocolate-covered peanut cluster, the other shining gold – accompanied by a letter from the anonymous sender who signed himself "the man who found Pegleg's black gold." The finder wrote to the magazine several times, and included a black-coated nugget with his correspondence to confirm his identity. Incidentally, the black coating was indeed oxidized copper, so Pegleg hadn't lied about that.

If You Go

Anza-Borrego State Park: *The park headquarters is next to the town of Borrego Springs, north of Interstate 8 and west of Brawley and the Salton Sea. Developed campgrounds and primitive sites are both available. A resort hotel, gas, and restaurants are available in Borrego Springs, and all facilities are offered in the nearby cities. The park is 80 miles east of San Diego. ☎ (760) 767-5311.*

Pegleg Smith Monument: *East of Borrego Springs on the county road to Salton City. Beyond the airport, the highway makes a sharp left, then a mile later, a sharp right (at the intersection of Pegleg Road and Henderson Canyon). The monument is north of the road at this intersection. No telephone.*

Pegleg Smith's Gold: *If you find it, give me a call and I'll help load it for you.*

The Salton Sea

The land is biblical: miles of date palm tree orchards, the nearby hills barren and dry as a bone. The Salton Sea is a constant presence, with seagulls in the sky and a peculiar salt odor when the wind is right. There are much worse odors from decaying algae when conditions are wrong. The land seems alien and strange.

The Salton Sink

Prior to 1905, the Salton Sink was mired in a scientific controversy. Which was deeper – Death Valley or the Sink? Which was hotter? State and Federal cartographers, geologists, mineralogists, and meteorologists surveyed both areas, and opinions flew like tumbleweeds.

The Salton Sink stretches from Palm Springs to Mexicali, and it's one of the most developed areas on the California Desert. The Sink is now first-class agricultural land, growing citrus, figs, and several other warm-weather crops. It's the Colorado River and a complex system of irrigation ditches that make this possible.

The Salton Sink is a traditional home and endpoint for the Colorado River. Numerous times in ages past the river has flowed here; it has formed lakes, then changed its course. The lakes then dried up, returning the bottom of the sink to the desert. As recently as 400 years ago, Lake Cahuilla covered a much larger area than the current Salton Sea. On the hillsides above the Sea the level of the previous lake forms a beach line, and there are numerous fish traps left by the Cahuilla Indians.

Colorado Desert

Record-Breaking Facts

This is one of the hottest and lowest places in the world.

Death Valley, which currently holds the record as the hottest place in the Western Hemisphere, did not always have that distinction. The Salton Sink held that record in the late 1800s and early 1900s. At the Mammoth Tank Station on the Southern Pacific Railroad the temperature hit 126°, a record not beaten until the heat wave of 1913 drove the temperature at Furnace Creek to 134°.

The method of determining elevation that was used – it was based on barometric measurements – kept the question of which area was deeper hotly contested. During the last half of the 1800s, surveyors proclaimed the bottom of Death Valley to be anywhere from 480 feet to 275 feet below sea level. The Salton Sink rose and sank also, but not by as much, varying from 215 to 275 feet below sea level. Neither location reaches as far down as the Dead Sea, the surface of which is 1,292 ft below sea level.

Death Valley's official lowest elevation is 282 feet below sea level, near Badwater. The record is safe now. The surface of the Salton Sea is 228 feet below sea level.

The Salton Sea is now a more or less permanent fixture of the Colorado Desert, since about as much water drains into it as is lost each year to evaporation. It is 360 square miles, 35 miles long, with 110 miles of shoreline, and is popular with Southern California's fishermen and boaters.

The Accident that Created the Salton Sea

The Sea was born by accident in 1905.

Before the turn of the century, a California dreamer by the name of **Charles R. Rockwood** saw the possibilities of bringing water to the

Conchilla (now known as the Coachella Valley; the original name was the Spanish word for little shells) and Imperial valleys from the Colorado River. He saw that a canal could be dug south of Yuma, cross about 60 miles of Mexican desert, and deliver enough water to transform the region into a rich agricultural center. With another developer – Anthony Heber – he formed the **California Development Company** in 1896. They had difficulties raising enough money, but were able to cut a few corners and began to build their canal in 1902. But the corner-cutting cost them, as the canal was plagued with silting problems and was not built to withstand a flood, which was bound to occur. In 1905 the Red Bull went on a rampage.

The breach was so major that the entire flow of the Colorado – at flood stage – was diverted into the Salton Sink. Engineers from the California Development Company were unable to handle the repairs. The Southern Pacific Railroad stepped in, since many miles of track and their major connection to Southern California was in jeopardy. With a major effort, they repaired the break, only to have it split again, and the mighty Colorado continued to flow into the valley. The railroad gave up; the financial panic of 1906 made other matters more pressing. But President Theodore Roosevelt stepped in and convinced the railroad to try again. The American government couldn't do the job, for reasons of politics and money; the breach was in Mexico and no treaty was in place that would allow the United States to work there. Besides, the agencies that would be responsible did not have the funds and Congress was not likely to provide them. The railroad engineers and workers, making a truly heroic effort, eventually made the repairs.

But the damage was done. The Salton Sea was filled. Salton City was under water, as were a salt plant and hundreds of acres of prime agricultural land. An inland sea was born from the desert, a sea that remains as controversial as its birth.

Too Much Salt, Too Little Oxygen

"I like to say that the Sea is an 'island' in the desert," says Steve Horvitz, the Superintendent of the Salton Sea State Recreation Area. Horvitz is concerned about the future of the Salton Sea, as it is embroiled in a new political and scientific controversy. The sea itself is continually degrading. The problem is threefold: salt, oxygen, and nutrients. This problem – and that chronic sore point in California, water and how it should be used – is a looming environmental catastrophe.

The water of the Salton Sea is continually replenished by irrigation and waste water. About 1.3 million acre-feet of water are added each year. The irrigation water comes from the Colorado River, which is naturally salty; it picks up salt as it passes through the Coachella and Imperial valleys as well. Additionally, the soil of the desert is alkaline, and when the lake was born a great deal of salinity was leached out of the soil into the water.

There is no outlet from the Salton Sea; any water that leaves does so by evaporation only. When the water evaporates, it leaves the salt behind, which increases the alkalinity of the remaining water. The amount of salt in the water increases about four million tons each year. Presently, the level of dissolved salt in the Sea is around 43 parts per thousand. The Pacific Ocean is around 35 parts.

"We expect that, as the level of salt in the Sea approaches 45 parts, some of the fish will stop reproducing," according to Horvitz, "and by the time that it reaches 60 parts most of the sport fish will have disappeared from the Sea. Left unchecked, the salt levels will increase to the point that the present systems will no longer be able to exist. This process is natural and it would be very difficult to stop."

This would not be a critical environmental issue, as it is a part of the natural process of the desert; lakes form, by whatever means, and they dry up. The Salton Sink has done so in the past. But Horvitz points out that the Salton Sea has become an important stop for migrating birds. Hundreds of thousands of birds have come to depend upon the Sea's abundant fish for food.

"Three hundred eighty species of birds have been counted at the Sea," according to Horvitz. "This is close to half of the total species known to exist in the United States. Imagine that. Almost half of the species of birds that exist in our country have been seen at the Sea! Millions of birds use the Sea each winter day! There's more bird and wildlife diversity here than any other place in California, maybe the nation. If the birds no longer found the high level of food that currently exists at the Sea, available nutrition for their reproductive needs would decrease; stresses would increase. Mortality among juveniles would rise and adult fish-eating birds would be forced to find and use other habitat."

Why does this matter? Because there is nowhere else for them to go.

And here we hit the heart of the efforts behind the reason to stabilize the Sea's salt level, according to Horvitz. "We have consumed our wetlands throughout Southern California. Our coastal riparian areas now host our buildings and roads; the Colorado River is mostly channelized and homes lace its shore. We have done very well at building homes and infrastructure for us – not so well at preserving a part of nature that is so important for all of us. If the Sea can no longer support the bird population because there are no fish, because the salt has increased to the point that they don't reproduce, many of the birds that use this lake will no longer be able to survive here."

However, there is a problem that may be even more imminent than the salt content – oxygen, and the effects that heat and nutrients have upon the oxygen content of the water here.

Oxygen, of course, is essential to the fish, and the fish are essential to the birds. Temperature affects the amount of available oxygen in water; cold water holds more, hot water much less. So on very hot days the amount of oxygen in the water is reduced. But even more dangerous is the mix of nutrients and plant life.

Nutrients from agricultural water and from treated sewer plant discharges are in the irrigation water that enters the Salton Sea. These nutrients feed the algae found in the lake. While the brown algae does not seem to cause a problem, the green algae does. A big influx of nutrients can set off a green algae bloom – a condition that leads to serious oxygen depletion.

"Great portions of the lake will experience algal blooms," according to Horvitz. "The Sea turns green, or brown, and sometimes small portions even show a reddish color when algal species bloom. I've seen the Sea turn bright green in a matter of hours as the plant life bursts into action, spurred on by nutrients. When this happens, you better hang on to your hat, or run for the hills. Because the algae will bloom and quickly die. When they die they pull oxygen from the wa-

Colorado Desert

ter of the Sea. So much so that, more often than not, not enough oxygen remains to sustain the fish, and large-scale fish die-offs will follow within a day or so."

Horvitz adds, "We know from our tests that the oxygen profiles of the Sea during these periods are dramatic. Sometimes only the first inch or so of water has oxygen in it. Often below a meter or two we find no dissolved oxygen. So we see the fish at the surface of the lake gulping for air."

Horvitz says that "The algae that tend to turn the water a green color are the ones that give us trouble, often cause fish die-offs, and produce an unpleasant odor. These species bloom with abundance in appropriate conditions. They die quickly, taking with them the oxygen and causing the fish to struggle. Fishing is generally poor during periods of green algal blooms."

This oxygen deficiency causes fish die-offs in large numbers. Horvitz believes it is just a matter of time until there is a catastrophic event in which most or all of the fish in the lake die.

"I believe that the system will experience a catastrophic event within a matter of several years, due in part to the excessive nutrient load. When it does, fish will die outright. They will not simply stop reproducing, as in the case of high salt levels. They will die by the millions, float to the surface and wash ashore. This is beginning to happen as we have more algal blooms that cause localized ecosystem collapses. These local events seem to get bigger year by year. I think we will see the big one happen pretty soon."

Horvitz continues, "Both the salt and nutrient load problems are very serious. Both must be addressed. Failing to reduce the Sea's nutrient level but reducing its salt load may only give us a less salty lake that fish and birds die in. Reducing the nutrient level and not addressing the salt will give us a lake facing a system devoid of fish, and then fish-eating birds. This will probably have a devastating affect on the migrating bird populations in the Western states. Both issues have to be addressed for a healthy Sea."

The Demand for Water

As serious as the nutrient loading and the increasing salt content are, there is another storm cloud on the horizon, one that could bring about the end of the Salton Sea. That problem is the ever-growing demand for water throughout California.

Presently, there is a balance between evaporation loss and the incoming stream of water. But water districts throughout Southern California are casting greedy eyes on the 1.3 million acre-feet the Sea needs, and they may get it – or a substantial portion. As much as 575,000 acre-feet could be lost in the near future to new claims.

"The water is essential for the survival of the Sea," according to Horvitz. "If 575,000 acre-feet of water is removed annually from the Sea, the salinity and nutrient loading problems will be aggravated, hastening the collapse of essential biological systems."

Whether the Salton Sink returns to desert or remains one of the largest lakes and migratory bird sanctuaries on the American continent is a political football. It is a fascinating spot. While it is populous and developed, there are several places here worth the time to visit, and it's a curious place – almost foreign, unlike any other desert area in America.

If You Go

Palm Springs, Palm Desert, etc. – these towns are famous for golf, movie stars, and big-ticket homes. Almost everyone chooses to cruise through here once to see how the other half lives. After the obligatory tour, there are some worthwhile sights in the immediate area, and the farther you get away from the freeway, the better it gets. Brawley and El Centro are in the center of the Colorado, and some very interesting and beautiful desert areas are nearby.

The Palm Springs Desert Museum, ☎ (760) 325-0189, is well worth a visit. It's open 10 to 5 except Fridays (open till 8 pm) and Mondays, when it is closed. The museum is off Palm Canyon Drive (California Highway 111), south of Tramway Road. The Tramway, which takes passengers to

Colorado Desert

the top of the San Jacintos, gives spectacular views of the desert.

*The **Living Desert Reserve** is a park with several miles of nature trails and some very interesting natural exhibits. The reserve is in Palm Desert, on Portola Avenue about 1½ miles south of Palm Canyon Drive. It is closed during August, and hours vary with the season. Call the Reserve at ☎ 619-346-5694.*

*__Salton Sea__: The State Recreation Area, ☎ (760) 393-3052, is on the western shore of the lake. A large wildlife refuge is on the south shore. **Anza-Borrego State Park**, ☎ (760) 767-5311, is southwest of the Sea.*

North of Yuma

The mighty Colorado is tame now; a series of dams keep its water under check. The dams use the water to generate electricity, then force it into ditches and pipes for delivery to cities and farms. Much of the river is a huge playground for water skiers and fishermen. For miles the flood plain is farmed, although large areas are also held in reserve as wildlife refuges. In the south, the river has turned an exceptionally interesting desert into miles of alfalfa and carrots. But between the bluffs west of Yuma and the Algodones Dunes – also called the Imperial Dunes – some fine desert remains, some of the hottest but most scenic country there is.

It wasn't hot early in the morning on the first day of April, when we left Yuma after a day of clouds spitting rain. This was one of the few rainstorms the city experiences, and we were fortunate enough to be there for it. The air was washed clean, the sky crystal blue. If the watercourses were not full – they probably wouldn't be, as the rain had stopped the night before – I knew the sandy washes should be in good shape. If they were dry enough to drive, then the sand would be firm and there'd be less risk of getting stuck.

So we struck out west, then north.

North of Interstate 8 on Ogilby Road is an old mining area known as the **Gold Rock Mining District**. Here, in the Cargo Muchacho (loosely translated from Spanish as "Loaded Boy") Mountains, was a booming mining town known as Hedges and later as **Tumco**, from the initials of The United Mines Company. From 1870 to 1909 as many as 3,000 people lived and worked here. Now only the cemeteries remain. According to local legend, the Spanish first found gold in

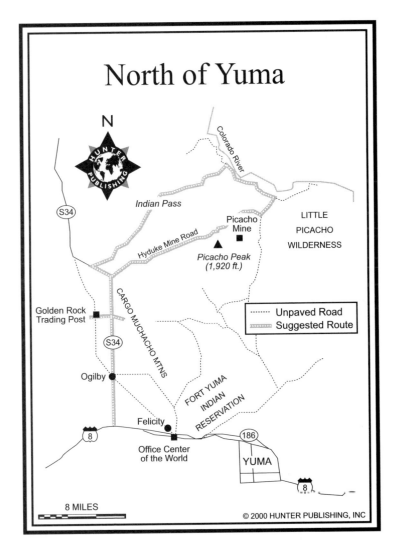

these mountains in the 1820s. The Cargo Muchachos were reportedly named when two boys left a nearby Spanish encampment to explore one of the canyons, and returned with their pockets loaded with gold ore. But the Spanish did not develop any mines here; the first mining activity came with the Americans in 1870.

A mile or two south of the vacant townsite is an interesting-looking place, the **Gold Rock Trading Post**, but it's closed. It's reported to have a fine collection of rocks, books on the desert, and antique mining equipment, but a visit inside will have to wait for another trip. We head on, northward. The **Algodones Dunes** – or Imperial Dunes, depending on your preference – stretched west of the road, running more or less parallel to it, as far as we can see.

The Algodones Dunes.

Exploring the Picacho Peak Region

Beyond Gold Rock and Tumco a couple of four-wheel-drive trails can take us back to the Colorado River, and to an old mining district that was serviced by steam-powered river boats in the 1800s. The Picacho Peak region is now a state recreation area, but was once a wide-open, wild and woolly mining center, and a significant amount of gold was taken out of those hills. Zane Grey lived here for a while, and set one of his classic Westerns – *Wanderer of the Wasteland* – here. It is a beautiful and rugged area, still remote, and if the rains hadn't washed out the roads, we were going to see it.

Two roads take off from Ogilby Road to the **Picacho Peak Recreation Area**. The **Hyduke Mine Road** heads due east to the spires of Picacho Peak itself; according to the maps, it's a four-wheel-drive trail, the kind I like. **Indian Pass Road** wanders more northward before reaching the river and following it south to Hyduke Mine Road. Unfortunately, there was water on the Hyduke Road, and a look-over of the trail ahead convinced us that wisdom might be the better part of valor, so we chose the Indian Pass Road.

It was a great choice, if only for the scenery. Indian Pass is breathtaking.

The road to the pass is dirt, but smooth, well-bladed, and suited for a passenger car. A few miles down the road some snowbirds were parked in their motorhomes, camped about a quarter-mile off the road.

The vegetation here is sparse. Here are ocotillos, teddy bear cholla, small bushes of creosote, and an occasional barrel cactus; smoke trees and desert acacias line the washes. The soil is a sandy gravel, a strange mix of volcanic rock and clay from the land's distant past as the delta of the Colorado. The mountains are predominately chocolate-brown but other colors mix in. Yellow, red, green and blue appear at odd times, in layers; the various soils and rocks lie in sheets tilted and faulted by the geologic forces that built this land. The road is smooth and easy.

Cholla cactus.

Ocotillo cactus.

Smooth and easy, that is, to the top of the pass. As we climb, a beautiful vista emerges, a vista of the mountains that piled up to keep the Colorado River caged and away from this desert. Ahead and on the left is the Indian Pass Wilderness, and to our right, the Picacho Peak Wilderness.

A cold wind is blowing at the summit and the day is incredibly beautiful. Puffs of clouds are in the western sky. The bladed road ends at the summit, with a wide spot for camping and enjoying the view. A rocky four-wheel-drive trail takes off down the other side, and so do we, heading down to a wash that looks empty and dry. The road is rough but passable in a high-clearance vehicle; I put it in four-wheel first for the fun of it, then for need as we twisted our way down.

Gavilan Wash gradually widens from a canyon to a desert river. While the sand is still moist from the rains, tire tracks on the road show that the rain had not been enough to make the water run; it's safe, but we proceed carefully. Smoke trees and Palo Verde grow well here, and their shade would be welcome on a summer day. We pass some evidence of past mining activity; someone found something, but it wasn't much, as the diggings are more a prospect hole than a mine.

Now we find signs. We're at the Picacho Peak State Recreation Area. It's a remote region and it's a comfort to know there is a ranger around. The wash we're driving down widens, and ahead is the Colorado River.

The trail becomes a road, and suddenly we're at a junction. The river is hidden behind a field of reeds and trees and the road becomes a muddy mess. The campground is eight miles south, but from the mud we've already encountered it's an eight miles we don't want to cover. It's time to turn around.

Driving out, up the wash, we can feel a sense of the ordeal our fore-bears went through, coming to California on the southern route. They'd crossed many, many miles of harsh dry country, wild and untamed, a country with angry, unwelcoming natives. Coming to the Colorado was a major milestone. But ahead the country was even drier than the land they had already covered, and it happened imme-diately – with no transition, they were back in it, back on the hot, dry desert where the slightest error could mean death. It's a lonely land, here in the most remote corner of California, and a land that can't be tamed.

Thank God for that. I want my children to come here, and their chil-dren, to reach inside themselves and find they have the courage to overcome the challenges and changes of such a strange and hostile environment. I want them to learn the lessons of the smoke tree and the creosote; to adjust to the changes of fortune, adapt to the world around them, and sink deep enough roots that they can survive any dry spell, weather any storm.

The Center of the World

Felicity, California, is a townsite a few miles west of Yuma, Ari-zona, along Interstate 8. It's a small place, and very young – incorpo-rated in 1986. It hasn't grown much since. Its founder is a French-born American, Jacques-André Istel, who served in the US Marines during the Korean War. In 1952 he became enchanted by the desert. He moved there when he retired from business in 1985, and named the community for his wife Felicia. To promote his town, and fix it forever with a unique place in the great scheme of things, he came up with an unusual approach. He wrote a children's book that declared his town was the center of the world.

His book *Coe the Good Dragon at the Center of the World* – settles any argument about the location of the center of the world; it's his town, period. The book was a success, and the supervisors of Impe-rial County were proud of it. They proclaimed that Felicity was indeed The Official Center of the World. In 1989, the government of France followed suit. Their Institut Géographique National recognized Felicity as the Official Center of the World.

Istel next sought a way to use the town's celebrity status. If all goes according to Istel's plan, the Center will eventually have a hundred granite walls as memorials, filled with the names of significant people of our time. The Wall for the Ages is already built, as is the Marine Corps Korean Wall Memorial bearing the names of 4,617 Marines and 107 Navy corpsmen who died in the Korean War.

If You Go

Felicity and the **Official Center of the World** *are nine miles west of Yuma on Interstate 8. Take the Sidewinder exit to the frontage road north of the freeway, then turn west. The village features the Granite Wall of the Ages, a 21-foot-tall pyramid, a section of the Eiffel Tower Stairs, and a Sundial with Michelangelo's "Arm of God." For more information* ☎ *619-572-0100.*

Gold Rock *and* **Tumco** *are about 22 miles northwest of Yuma. Take Interstate 8 west to Ogilby Road exit and drive north for nine miles. Tumco was once known as Hedges, and may be listed that way on some maps. If you do any exploring in the area be aware of mine shafts. Local residents say that some of them go straight down as much as 1,000 feet.*

Picacho Peak*: The BLM has set aside large parts of this area for recreation, and the State of California Park Service has a campground along the river. It can be accessed either by the two trails off Ogilby Road (Hyduke Mine or Indian Pass) or from Winterhaven. Ogilby Road is County Road S34, which connects Interstate 8 and State Highway 78.*

The Blythe Intaglios

The Blythe Intaglios are a surprise and a mystery. While there we found another surprise.

The intaglios are north of Blythe on Highway 95. A visit isn't particularly satisfying; all we saw were fences and BLM signs. To see the intaglios we'd have to be in an airplane well above the desert sand. That is how they were discovered. An airplane pilot, George Palmer, observed them in 1930.

The Intaglios are figures made by Native Americans perhaps as much as 1,100 years ago. They are huge: the largest is about 171 feet long and 158 feet wide. There is a figure of a woman, a serpent, and a four-legged animal, which some believe is a horse. If it is a horse, that would date the intaglios to the time after the arrival of the Spanish. But others say this figure is an animal from Mojave Indian creation legend, and radiocarbon dating techniques suggest the Intaglios were in fact made around 890 A. D.

Whatever they are, the bigger mystery is why. Why did these Native Americans make figures that could only be seen from the air?

Behind the intaglios, which are fenced for protection, is a hill with a steep trail leading to its peak. We climb it and park near a yellow Jeep. A couple inside were examining the intaglios, and we got out to see what we could see – which, as far as the intaglios is concerned, was nothing. The view of the Colorado River was stunning, and the mountains of Arizona beyond were calling my name; but the ancient figures could not be discerned from this altitude.

The couple with the Jeep were Gerald and Janel Eckles, from Yucaipa. They have a trailer on the river a few miles to the east, and spent their vacation time either boating on the Colorado or four-wheeling on the desert around Blythe. They'd been back in the hills – the Big Marias – and were taking a break on the hilltop overlooking the intaglios before heading home.

They'd found a mine back in the hills, probably a gold mine, in the first rise of the mountains behind us. They pointed out the hill: a

Colorado Desert

steep bluff, with tailings and workings on its summit, about three miles away. They'd been coming to the mine for a few years. About two years ago they noticed yellow flowers on a flat area some distance above the wide spot where they'd parked. The flowers were a curiosity, as almost nothing could grow in the brown rock tailings above.

They hiked up to the flowers and found they were big plastic sunflowers, tied to a wooden cross. The cross was two stakes wired together and was placed at the head of a rock-covered grave. About 10 or 15 feet from the grave was a flat marble marker. When they cleaned off the marker, there was a picture of a bearded old man cut in the left side, a map of the river in the center, and a picture of an older woman on the right. Across the bottom were the words, "Wyatt Earp's Trails End."

Trail's End.

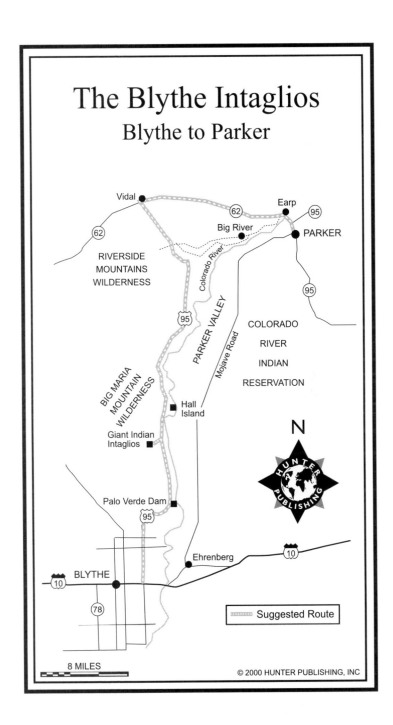

The Blythe Intaglios
Blythe to Parker

Vidal

Earp

62

95

Big River

PARKER

62

RIVERSIDE
MOUNTAINS
WILDERNESS

Colorado River

95

95

PARKER VALLEY

COLORADO

Mojave Road

RIVER

INDIAN

RESERVATION

BIG MARIA
MOUNTAIN
WILDERNESS

Hall
Island

Giant Indian
Intaglios

N

Palo Verde Dam

95

Ehrenberg

10

BLYTHE

10

78

xxxxxxx Suggested Route

8 MILES

© 2000 HUNTER PUBLISHING, INC

Colorado Desert

》———————————————《

Wyatt Earp

Probably no one in the Old West is more controversial, or more studied, than Wyatt Earp. Depending on the authority, he was a cold-blooded killer and itinerant gambler whose lucky streaks were a little too good; or he was the greatest lawman in the history of the West, who stood up to evil and shot it down. He was a hard businessman with a sharp eye for profit and an entrepreneur who was very lucky. He may have been a humorless bully, according to some; others say he had the sort of humor that Westerners are expected to have – dry, understated, and either you get it or you don't.

Most agree that he was a taciturn man who let his actions speak for him. And he certainly was lucky; in all his gunfights – and unlike some Western folk heroes, he had many – he was never wounded, not once.

After the Shootout at the OK Corral and its aftermath, including a trial that cleared him, his brothers, and Doc Holiday of murder charges, Earp moved west with his wife Josephine (known as Sadie). He went to Alaska, then California and, unlike most other gunslingers, died a natural death as an old man in 1929 near Los Angeles.

He spent his time in the endeavors that suited him best; he worked as a lawman and a gambler, and pursued business interests that included saloons and mines. He's reported to have owned as many as 100 claims, mostly in the Whipple Mountains to the north. He lived in Vidal, which is the next wide spot in the road north of here, and for a while in a town now called Earp, near Parker.

》———————————————《

We Visit the Mine

It didn't take much to convince the Eckles they could make another trip to the mine today. Gerald and Janel were true Jeepers and any excuse was welcome to go back into four-wheel drive. We started out down the hill, much to Dally's delight.

Dally has become a desert dog on these trips. She gets the back seat, but shares it with camera gear and those desert books that seem to accumulate every time we stop at a park or store. The hill is very steep, so steep that once we start down there's no turning back, nor could we stop if we had to. With the sand and the angle, once we started down we were going all the way, even when Dally slid off the seat and onto the floor.

Only her pride was damaged, though; she's a tough old dog, and as we took off

Dally.

across the barren gravel and rock northward she climbed back up, shook off her shame, and settled in to enjoy the trip.

We wandered up the pole line road from the intaglios, then west along a trail that quickly degenerated into a pair of fresh tracks. It was the wrong road, and Gerald led us off cross-country, over gullies and rocks, then back to the pole line road. More than a little embarrassed, he stopped and explained that we'd missed the turn. But, with all the wrong turns I've taken, and my propensity for making short trails long, I wasn't about to be concerned.

But the pole line road – which usually is a main highway on any desert – wasn't typical; it hadn't been bladed in a number of years, and was as rough as any desert trail. We hit a washout. The little Jeep buzzed through it but our Cherokee slammed to a stop, wheels churning dirt, and rocks sliding out from under us.

Dally wasn't impressed, and Suz was upset. She hates it when we get stuck. After a few attempts, we realized my front wheels weren't getting power; I blessed the memory of Dave Hughes out on the Mojave Trail. After kicking myself for not permanently fixing the problem back home, I got out, crawled under the front of the Jeep, and re-attached the vacuum line that had fallen off once again. We climbed out of the washout easily.

We followed the little jeep into the hills, entered another dry wash, then climbed the side of a mountain. The drop on our right was impressive; probably not a fatal one, but not a direction we'd want to take. The trail was low-range, first-gear slow, not the least of which was due to a blind hairpin corner that we took only because we could see the little yellow Jeep ahead of us had successfully negotiated the turn. At last we stopped on a bench. The view was magnificent. The Colorado River lay at our feet. Arizona beckoned.

We climbed to the marker, and there it was, a small memento to history and the strange, silent man who had helped tame the West. The legends of Wyatt Earp came to mind, legends that overpower whatever facts shaped his life; we could smell the faint whiff of gunsmoke, hear the chips lightly clink as they fall together on the green felt-covered table, taste the raw burn of cheap whiskey. Here had been the man that did his part to change the West from a lawless, brutal hangout for murderers and crooks, allowing the clerks and engineers to live safely in their homes and build the industries that made the land habitable. Whether he had been a brutal bully or a misunderstood force for right who could not articulate his feelings, he was a man who did a job that needed to be done.

The stop at Trail's End was a fitting one. Here this trail ends, and another begins. There are a lot of places on the California desert we skipped by in our desert dancing tour. Come see them for yourself, and discover your secrets here. For me, Arizona is calling. I'm there. See you on the trail.

If You Go

Blythe Intaglios: *These are about 15 miles north of Blythe on Highway 95. The BLM has posted signs next to the highway that lead to the markers.*

Trail's End: *This trail is difficult to find – follow these directions at your own risk. It is a difficult four-wheel-drive trail with a steep grade and a hairpin turn that is a little scary.*

The mine road takes off westward from the pole line road next to the highway, at a distance of two miles north of the BLM access road to the intaglios. Follow the mine road for three miles. You'll enter a wash, and the road splits; follow the trail on the right, and climb the hill to the south. The mine is near GPS coordinates 33° 48.73' and 114° 34.62'.

Colorado Desert

Appendix I

Websites & Addresses

Websites

www.desertdancing.com. This is my site, with links to other sites about the desert.

www.desertusa.com. *DesertUSA* is an excellent online magazine about deserts.

www.off-road.com. This is a huge site, an online magazine about four-wheeling and off-road vehicles, with numerous trail reports and all kinds of vehicle information. It also offers a Western Mojave trail guide.

www.outdoorwire.com. The Outdoor Recreation Network. There is a section dedicated to 4x4 trails, with complete descriptions of routes and remote places to visit on the North American deserts.

www.fieler.com/ballarat. Ballarat Ghost town.

www1.ridgecrest.ca.us/~matmus/default.html. Matarango Museum.

www.calparksmojave.com. Mojave Desert State Parks.

www.mdhca.org. Mojave Desert Heritage and Cultural Association

www.ca.blm.gov/caso. Official site for the Bureau of Land Management.

www.ca.blm.gov/barstow. Bureau of Land Management Barstow office.

www.death.valley.national-park.com. Official site for Death Valley National Park.

www.nps.gov/moja. Official site for the Mojave National Preserve.

www.nps.gov/jotr/. Official site for Joshua Tree National Park.

http://ceres.ca.gov/ceres/calweb/deserts.html. CERES is an Internet information system developed by the California Resources Agency (State of California). The website contains good information about the California deserts.

Federal Land Management & Park Offices on the Mojave

Mojave National Preserve

Mojave National Preserve Desert Information Center
72157 Baker Blvd./ PO Box 241
Baker, CA 92309
☎ 760-733-4040
E-mail: MOJA_Baker_Interp@nps.gov

Mojave National Preserve Desert Information Center
707 W. Broadway
Needles, CA 92363
☎ 760-326-6322
E-mail: MOJA_Needles_Interp@nps.gov

Superintendent
Mojave National Preserve
222 E. Main Street, Suite 202
Barstow, CA 92311
☎ 760-255-8801

National Parks

Call ☎ 800-365-2267 to reserve campsites in any national park.

Death Valley National Park
PO Box 579
Death Valley, CA 92328
☎ 760-786-2331

Joshua Tree National Park
74485 National Park Drive
29 Palms, CA 92277
☎ 760-367-5500

Bureau of Land Management Desert Area Field Offices

California Desert Information Center
831 Barstow Road
Barstow, CA 92311
☎ 760-252-6060

Barstow Field Office
2601 Barstow Road
Barstow, CA 92311
☎ 760-252-6000; Fax: 760-252-6099

Needles Field Office
101 W. Spikes Road
Needles, California 92363
☎ 760-326-7000; Fax: 760-326-7099

Bakersfield Field Office
3801 Pegasus Drive
Bakersfield, CA 93308-6837
☎ 805-391-6000; Fax: 805-391-6040

Appendix

Palm Springs South Coast Field Office
690 Garnet Ave, PO Box 1260
Palm Springs, CA 92258
☎ 760-251-4800; Fax: 760-251-4899

El Centro Field Office
1661 S. 4th St.
El Centro CA, 92243
☎ 760-337-4400; Fax: 760-337-4490

BLM Open Areas
(Off-Highway Vehicle Areas)

The sites below are set aside for open, unrestricted cross-country travel. Here is a list of the areas and the office responsible for them. (Office contact information is given above.)

Barstow Office

Dumont Dunes, San Bernardino County
El Mirage, San Bernardino County
Johnson Valley, San Bernardino County
Juniper Flats, San Bernardino County
Rasor, San Bernardino County
Stoddard Valley, San Bernardino County

El Centro Office

Plaster City Open Area, Imperial County
Superstition Open Area, Imperial County
Imperial Sand Dunes, Imperial County
Lark Canyon Off-Highway Vehicle Area, San Diego County

Appendix II

Desert Travel

Land Use

The desert is mostly public land. While there is a lot of private property, most of the millions of acres are owned by us. Some of these areas are military reservations to which access is not permitted. Otherwise, much of the rest is administered by the US Bureau of Land Management or the National Park Service, and access is allowed. The rules for access will depend upon whose land it is (the Park Service is usually more restrictive than the BLM) and the type of land use that has been designated.

The type of land use allowed will normally be posted. We have to keep vehicles out of closed or **Wilderness** areas, unless there is a designated travel corridor. In open areas, we can follow the trails and can park or camp within 300 feet of the roadway. It's always a good idea to stay on the trail, or as close to it as possible, to avoid damaging the environment. Throughout much of the desert, the Bureau of Land Management requires that vehicles remain on established trails and paths, except for setting up camp.

Open **OHV Play Areas** are special lands set aside to allow unlimited access. OHV Parks are a relatively new concept for the Bureau of Land Management. These areas are used by the more radical off-roaders; travel is completely unrestricted and the tougher, the better. The idea was to limit off-road travel to these areas, and keep vehicles on the established trails in all other areas of the desert, thus keeping the environmental destruction to a minimal area. The jury is still out on whether this is an intelligent plan. Concentrating the dirt bikes, jeeps, and all-terrain vehicles in small enclaves means there is a lot of destruction in those areas, instead of minor or insignificant erosion throughout the desert.

These OHV parks are relatively safe places to try out your new four-wheel-drive, gain faith in the off-road capabilities of your vehicle, learn off-road driving skills, or just mess around for a few hours. Usually, rangers from the BLM patrol these parks regularly so, unlike the rest of the desert, help is around if you get into major trouble.

There are some areas in which any motor vehicle is not allowed, and there are some mining claims, ranches, and private property, all of which will be posted and must be avoided. But a little respect and common courtesy, as well as common sense, will go a long way.

One thing to remember is that there is constant pressure from environmental groups to close these wonderful lands to all vehicle access. To keep from giving the Sierra Club any more reasons to act, we all need to Tread Lightly, and leave nothing but tracks. We also need to keep an eye on future trail closures, and do our part to protect our right of access. The people who oppose vehicular access to public lands are politically active. We have to be active too if we want to keep our right to visit public lands.

Desert Driving Tips

If you want to get off the pavement and onto the sand, you need four-wheel-drive, and the tougher, the better. Whatever vehicle you choose to drive out there, make sure it's in good condition and has good trail tires. Pay attention to your vehicle. It is your lifeline in and out of the desert. Driving technique is equally important. Here are some basic tips:

- ◈ Drive slow and easy. You'll damage tires, break things, run over desert tortoises, and lose out on experiences if you drive too fast.

- ◈ Stay on the top of, not in, the ruts. The exception is when driving in sand. In these conditions, try to keep the wheels where the sand is packed from the previous vehicles. When in sand, keep your speed up and use higher gears, don't spin the tires, and don't stop till you're clear of it.

◈ Put your vehicle in four-wheel-drive before you need it, and shift to low range early to reduce the strain on your vehicle.

◈ When you're approaching a hill, don't just rush into it blindly. Look it over, remembering that any hill you go down you may also have to come back up. If you don't think you can come back up it, don't go down, unless there is another clear and obvious trail out.

Make sure your vehicle is in top condition for desert travel.

Gear & Clothing

Every trip on the desert is an opportunity for, well, adventure, especially if I'm driving. Some adventures are worse than others. The desert can kill and it is no place to take chances. Be prepared for any emergency. I pack enough to survive at least two days.

The summer sun is the worst enemy you can have out there. Wear the proper clothing for the activity (sunglasses, hat, riding gear, sunscreen, wind breaker or long sleeved shirt for a change in the weather), and good walking shoes. It's a bad idea to wear shorts or a short-sleeved shirt; loose-fitting clothes (long pants and long sleeve shirt) will protect you from the sun and allow enough air circulation to help keep you cool. A hat helps keep the sun off your head.

Bees & Snakes

Be aware that a new animal threat is slowly making its way onto the desert. **Africanized honey bees** (killer bees) have been found on deserts from Texas to California. They aren't much different in size or appearance from regular bees, but seem to be mean as a grizzly with a bad tooth. The Internet magazine *Desert USA* (www.desertusa.com) has good information, which they update regularly, on killer bees. There is some good news about them: they have a range of a quarter-mile, so if attacked you can run that far and be out of their territory. They seem to target the face, so cover your face if attacked; consider carrying a homemade net just for that purpose, folded up and left in the pocket until needed.

Check *Desert USA*, local health agencies, and the BLM for the latest information and recommendations.

Rattlesnakes are another hazard of desert travel, especially in the spring and fall when they are coming and going from hibernation. If you make noise and watch where you step or put your hands, you may never see one. However, get the latest information on first-aid treatment before putting yourself at risk of being bitten.

Emergency Supplies

Aside from the usual tools – spare tire, jack, and so on – carry enough food and camping equipment to stay alive and relatively comfortable for several days in adverse conditions. I keep my emergency stores in a plastic carton in the garage, ready to be loaded first when I'm getting ready to hit the trail. In that carton are these supplies:

   ❖ First-aid kit – includes a snakebite kit (be sure to replace the rubber suction cups each spring), sunscreen, insect bite spray, burn ointment, Ace bandage, iodine, bandages, and Band-aids.

- ❖ Heat tablets – there's not much wood on the desert.

- ❖ MREs (Meals Ready to Eat) – they really aren't too bad if you're hungry enough. Army surplus stores have them.

- ❖ Spare compass, flashlight (check the batteries before you go), matches, pocket knife, spare blanket. I use one of those tiny aluminum emergency blankets you'll find in the sporting goods section. Who knows if they are any good, but they seem like a good idea.

- ❖ A gold pan (might get lucky) and a rock hammer.

- ❖ A small shovel, a tow rope, and two boards, each two feet long, in case you get stuck.

- ❖ Camping and emergency tools: aerial or road flares, rope or cord, duct or electrician's tape, small tarp or ground cover.

- ❖ Lots of fluids – I usually carry a gallon of water per person, plus an ice chest with Gatorade.

- ❖ A cell phone (they usually work in the desert areas).

- ❖ Maps – usually two or three of the same area, as they don't always agree.

- ❖ A fire extinguisher.

The last three items remain up front with me, close at hand. On longer four-wheeling back-country trips, additional supplies may be needed:

- ❖ Tire irons and an inner tube or an extra spare.

- ❖ Compressor or manual tire pump.

- ❖ Two gallons of water for the radiator.

- ❖ One gallon of engine oil.

- ❖ Five gallons of spare gas/diesel in a jerry can.

- ❖ Appropriate manuals for the vehicle to aid in trail-side repairs.

- ❖ Hi-Lift jack (or Jack-all), 48-inch minimum.

Desert Survival

Many people each year have mishaps in the desert that could have been avoided or made less serious with some preplanning. Here are some of the things you should do to avoid problems, and to deal with them if they come along.

◈ Before you leave, always let someone at home know your travel plans and a time when you will return. If you do get lost or break down, they will know where and when to start looking. Also, let these people know if your plans change. If there is no one at home to tell, then stop in at a ranger station or BLM office. Just be sure that you let them know when you are safely back from the desert.

◈ Learn about the area, get accurate maps and travel conditions, and plan your agenda conservatively if you are visiting an unfamiliar area. Remember that what may look like a short trip on the map may take many hours in four-wheel-drive, so allow enough time for safe travel. Also, know that a short trip by car can be a day-long hike. Plan accordingly; if you break down, you may need to hike out, assuming help doesn't come along.

◈ Know your limitations – don't plan extensive hikes or strenuous activity unless you are physically fit.

◈ Bring gear appropriate to your activity, the expected range of weather conditions and the planned length of your stay. Remember that conditions on the desert can change quickly, from a nice warm day to a rainstorm to a blizzard in a matter of hours.

If lost, stuck, or if you break down:

◈ Stay with your vehicle or otherwise make yourself visible.

◈ Keep calm – don't panic and don't waste time on "ifs" ("If only I hadn't done that… "). Spend your time constructively.

◈ Think through your options. Take stock of your supplies and situation.

◈ Stay put, unless you have a clear and specific destination.

◈ If you choose to hike out, avoid walking during the heat of the day; morning and evening walking is better for conserving your body's moisture. If you must leave your vehicle, leave a note telling the direction of your travel, your destination, and the date and time you left.

◈ Seek shelter from the elements, but try to make yourself visible (with smoke, a signal fire, or a brightly colored tarp).

Camping on the Desert

In addition to established campgrounds, the Bureau of Land Management allows dispersed camping in many areas, with a few limitations. Remember that the rules for travel and camping are different on National Park Service lands, which include the Mojave National Preserve.

BLM Camping Rules

These are the current rules and restrictions published by the BLM:

◈ The BLM allows dispersed camping up to 14 days at any one site. After 14 days, you must relocate to another site at least 25 miles away.

◈ When possible, use a BLM-established Dispersed Campsite. These can be found at the end of a spur road or a pullout, and are clear of vegetation and have a hard compacted surface. There may be a rock fire ring.

◈ Camps must be at least 600 feet away from any developed water source, so the water is available to wildlife and livestock. Camps should be at least 200 feet away from streams and springs.

◈ Park motorized vehicles within 300 feet of an established roadway, except in the open use areas.

◈ Camp only in designated campsites within the Rand Mountain-Fremont Valley Management Unit, and within Sage, Horse, and Cow Heaven canyons.

Appendix

- ✵ Pack it in, pack it out. Don't leave any litter – nothing but tracks.

- ✵ Leave Indian artifacts behind for others to enjoy.

- ✵ This is primitive camping, so do not trench or otherwise modify the ground or remove vegetation to "improve" the campsite. When possible, use an area that has been a campsite before. These sites will have been chosen because of good campsite conditions and accessibility.

- ✵ Avoid building new fire rings. If there is one near your chosen campsite, use it. Minimize the use and impact of fire. Keep fires small. Use only downed wood, or bring your own firewood as there is little available on the desert. Use a fire pan – a metal tray or garbage can lid to prevent the fire from blackening the soil. From May through October, there are seasonal fire restrictions in effect; fires must be kept small, in enclosed structures like barbecues or fire rings, and have at least 15 feet of clearance around the fire. A fire permit is required at these times. Permits can be obtained at any BLM office or state fire station. Keep in mind that, in extremely hot and dry conditions, second-stage fire restrictions may come into effect, allowing no open fires.

- ✵ If there are other campsites nearby, observe Quiet Time from 10 pm to 6 am. Be considerate to other campers in your area.

- ✵ Holding tanks or small "cat holes" are the recommendation for primitive "restrooms." It is illegal to dump holding tanks any place other than approved dump facilities. There is a safety and sanitary problem with digging large "latrine" holes. Stay with a one-hole-per-use plan and dig these shallow holes near vegetation and away from possible camping areas.

- ✵ Pack in what you need, and pack out your trash. Littering is not only inconsiderate to the next camper, but is illegal. As more people come up to enjoy desert camping, it becomes even more important to keep a clean area and leave your campsite in better condition than when you found it.

- ✵ If in doubt about where to camp, ask a ranger.

NPS Camping Rules

The rules are more restrictive when camping on land that is administered by the National Park Service (this includes Joshua Tree and Death Valley, as well as the Mojave National Preserve). Wildrose Station Ranger Dave Brenner provided the following guidelines in his e-mail newsletter for Death Valley visitors:

◈ **Off road driving**: Currently the park has numerous signs that state "Off-Road Driving Prohibited." These were placed back in the days of the monument and the intent of the sign was to keep vehicles on the existing roads. The park service has always enforced the prohibition on driving off a road onto a dry lake, for example, or driving off an existing road in search of a campsite.

This differs from the surrounding BLM (public) lands. Their definition allows for up to 300 feet of off-trail travel to locate a campsite (in limited use lands). Make sure that you have the latest DAG (desert access guide) for the area .

◈ **Road Corridors**: These are roads/trails that have been "carved" out of a wilderness area to allow motorized access. These corridors range from 30 feet from centerline on public lands to 50 feet on park dirt roads to a mile or more at the Saline Warm Springs. Each agency has different congressionally mandated corridor widths. They can be reviewed on the DPA blue line maps for Death Valley National Park, or at the BLM Ridgecrest/Bishop office or the Inyo National Forest Offices Lone Pine/Bishop California.

Most dirt backcountry roads are one lane. To pass, one should pick a spot that allows for the least impact on the surrounding environment or an area that will heal rapidly on the next rain. These tend to be washes or dry stream crossings.

◈ **Wilderness**: The park has a higher standard placed upon it legally and administratively. In general, wilderness places an "esthetic value on intrusions" such as noise, pets, motorized equipment and long-term impacts (group camps, etc.) which could impair one's perception and enjoyment of wilderness. Specific to wilderness, many roads were closed by the Desert Protection Act of '94. These closures to motorized access and pets are shown on maps of Death Valley. The same holds true for public BLM lands as well as National Forest lands with regard to motorized vehicles. However, pets are okay. Each resource or forest area and/or park area may impose a higher standard. One should contact the area agency for the most current information.

❖ **Trash**... what a concept. What is it? The desert is covered with the remains of many past peoples. This can range from a midden (native peoples' dump) to mine tailings, lumber, cans, glass bottles, arrowheads, cars, trucks, even airplanes. But if we take away what we carry in, i.e., "pack it in, and carry it out" or "take photos and leave shoe prints," then we will not impact the sites.

Items over 50 years old are protected by specific acts. If you want to remove anything, contact the agency on whose land the items are located for the proper guidance.

Ranger Brenner points out that trash has different meanings to different people, but that anything over 50 years old is protected – even if it is what we might think of as trash. He tells this story to make a point:

"I was with Phil Butler, a BLM ranger, when a man drove up with 10 trash bags full of tin cans and glass bottles. He wanted to know if he could give us the junk to throw away. We said sure, till we opened the bags. They were full of soldered cans and purple glass bottles. This good person had removed a layer of the past from an historic site without realizing the potential impact of his actions. We thanked him for his citizenship and educated him on the historical significance of such trash."

Thanks to Ranger Brenner for this information.

Appendix III

Mojave Desert State Parks

T he California State Park Service has done a notable job of preserving the heritage of the Mojave for future generations. These parks are usually rather small but well worth a visit. State rangers are devoted to understanding and preserving the Mojave, passing their knowledge on to desert adventurers, while preventing the wanton destruction of lands that has occurred in the past.

The California State Parks system maintains an excellent information center for the Western Mojave Desert in Lancaster, north of Los Angeles on Highway 14. This office manages Red Rock Canyon Saddleback Butte, Antelope Valley California Poppy Reserve, Antelope Valley Indian Museum, Tomo-Kahni, Ripley Desert Woodlands and Mitchell Caverns/Providence Mountains State Recreation Area. The rangers on duty are very helpful and informative.

The California State Parks/Mojave Desert Information Center is at 43779 15th St. West in Lancaster, CA off Hwy 14 at Ave K. Here you can find brochures, maps, and other information about parks and destinations in the Mojave Desert area. In addition to free materials, there is a store with very good books, as well as tourist stuff – T-shirts, sweatshirts, hats, maps, toys, and many additional items inspired by the Mojave Desert.

The **Mojave Desert Information Center** is open seven days a week from 9 am to 4 pm (except major holidays). Call the office at ☎ (805) 942-0662. The ranger on duty will answer questions about the state parks, give phone numbers and information about other state and local parks, and provide information about local federal agencies, including the National Park Service, Bureau of Land Management, Department of Defense – Edwards Air Force Base, and US Forest Service.

Red Rock Canyon State Park

We found Red Rock Canyon State Park to be one of the most beautiful places on the Mojave, and it is centrally located near several areas worth visiting on the western Mojave. It's on Highway 14, about 25 miles north of the city of Mojave. To the east are Randsburg and the El Paso Mountains, with Last Chance Canyon and Burro Schmidt's Tunnel to the north. There are off-highway vehicle parks to the north and south. Westward are the Sierras and the cool pines – a real blessing in summer.

Red Rock is a beautiful place but, like all desert canyons, it can be dangerous when a rainstorm hits. During the El Niño storms in the spring of 1998 a major flood wiped out not only large areas of the park and campground, it took out several hundred feet of Highway 14. Videos made of the flooding confirmed the wild nature of the storm and the huge wall of water that pounded down the canyon.

That flood was a reminder of one that stands tall in desert lore from a hundred years ago. On a dark, wild night, a wagon train hauling silver from the Cerro Gordo Mine camped in the canyon; it was one of the watering stops on the trail to Los Angeles. A flash flood came up, like the flood of 1998, that washed away several of the heavily laden wagons. At least one of them was never found, nor was any of the silver within.

It's a good story that keeps treasure hunters looking and hoping downstream from the canyon.

Antelope Valley
California Poppy Reserve

The desert is famous for its wildflowers, and the state has created the Antelope Valley California Poppy Reserve, ☎ (661) 942-0662, to protect and perpetuate outstanding displays of native wildflowers, particularly the California poppy. It's a display well worth seeing during the spring.

This 1,745-acre State Reserve, nestled in the Antelope Buttes, 15 miles west of Lancaster, California, is located on California's most consistent poppy-bearing land. Other wildflowers such as owl's clover, lupine, goldfield, cream cups, and coreopsis, to name only a few, produce a mosaic of color and fragrance each spring. The duration of the wildflower bloom, as well as its intensity, varies each year.

There are seven miles of trails, including a paved section for wheelchair access, that wind through the wildflower fields. Hillsides and fields of brilliant color make this park a fantastic place to visit.

Wildflowers bloom from March through May. The peak viewing period is mid-April. The visitor center is open March 15–May 1. There is a fee of $5 per vehicle to enter the park.

The Ripley Desert Woodland

The Ripley Desert Woodland, ☎ (661) 942-0662, is west of the Poppy Reserve on Lancaster Road at 210th Street West. This woodland isn't quite what Easterners and mountain people would expect; it's a forest, all right, but a forest of Joshua trees. Donated to the State by Arthur "Archie" Ripley, the park protects and preserves an impressive stand of native Joshuas and junipers, which once grew in great abundance throughout the Mojave. Today, only remnants of this desert forest remain in the Antelope Valley; the rest were cleared for farming and housing.

Appendix

Antelope Valley Indian Museum

The Antelope Valley Indian Museum, ☎ (661) 942-0662, is 15 miles east of Palmdale/Lancaster, on Avenue M, between 150th and 170th Street East. From Highway 14, go east on Avenue K or Palmdale Boulevard and follow the signs. The museum is closed during the summer months. It is open on weekends from 11 am to 4 pm from the middle of September through the middle of June.

The museum is housed in an unusual building that stands against towering rock formations in the Mojave Desert. Large boulders form the interior and timbers from Joshua trees cover supports for its roof.

The house was built by Howard Arden Edwards, an artist, who loved the desert scenery around the buttes. He envisioned a home that blended with the rock and sand. He homesteaded 160 acres on Piute Butte and in 1928 Edwards, his wife, and their son began building the home. He created a Swiss chalet that uses the butte and its boulders as an integral part of the building both inside and out.

Edwards was a collector of American Indian art and artifacts. The upper level of the home was designed solely as a display area for his collection of prehistoric and historic American Indian artifacts.

Grace Oliver, an anthropology student, bought the house, remodeled the main building, and added her own artifacts. She opened the Antelope Valley Indian Museum in the early 1940s and operated it for the next three decades, continuously adding to the collections. The State of California purchased the museum in 1979.

The museum has numerous displays and interpretive centers focused on the Southwestern, California and Great Basin Indians, although it contains artifacts from a number of other geographic regions.

It is an educational experience. The Joshua Cottage here features a touch table room where visitors can experience food-grinding techniques or learn how the Indians started a fire with a stick or bow drill.

Saddleback Butte State Park

Saddleback Butte State Park is a 3,000-acre preserve set aside for hiking and horseback riding. There are no off-road trails in the park. Hunting and shooting are also prohibited. Camping, hiking, bird watching, and photography are the primary activities. The park is located near the Antelope Valley Indian Museum. Saddleback Butte, elevation 3,651 feet, is a granite mountain that sits 1,000 feet above the Antelope Valley floor.

Wildlife viewing is good here. Bird watching is particularly popular, with golden eagles, hawks, ravens, and owls among the common predators. Smaller birds are spotted often: cactus wrens, thrashers, blackbirds, horned larks, woodpeckers, sparrows, and finches. There are desert tortoises, coyotes, kit foxes, rabbits, ground squirrels, kangaroo rats, badgers, skunks, and reptiles. Unfortunately, there are no more antelope. While the valley to the west was named for this spectacular animal, they've been driven out of the area permanently by human development.

Facilities include 25 picnic sites with tables and charcoal-wood stoves, each with ramadas for protection from the sun and wind. On the flatland, about a mile south of the butte, is a 50-unit family campground with tables, stoves and shade ramadas. There are flush toilets and water.

Horseback riding must be arranged in advance, as there is a locked gate to access the trail and no rangers are on the site. Call the state park office in Lancaster for information at ☎ 805-942-0662.

Mitchell Caverns & the Providence Mountains

Mitchell Caverns is in the heart of the Providence Mountains State Recreation Area, 60 miles west of Needles on Interstate 40. Spectacular and intricate limestone formations are found here, including stalagmites, stalactites, lily pads, draperies, curtains and popcorn. Desert prospector Jack Mitchell first explored the caves, then opened them up for public tours in 1932. The state bought the land and the Caverns in 1954.

Located at an elevation of 4,300 ft, temperatures usually remain moderate throughout the year. Temperatures inside the caverns are a constant, comfortable 65°.

Tours last about 1½ hours and are limited to 25 people. They cost $4 for adults and $2 for children six-17 (under age six are free). You are prohibited from exploring the caverns on your own. Call Mitchell Caverns in advance for reservations at ☎ 760-928-2586. Six campsites with tables and fire rings are available on a first-come, first-served basis.

Index

Adventuring in the California Desert (Foster), *142*
Afton Canyon, *58, 60*
Aguereberry, Pete, *115-116*
Aguereberry Point, *125-126*
Ahern, John, *84*
Algodones Dunes, *156*
animals, *see* wildlife
Antelope Valley, *3, 14-15, 50*
Antelope Valley California Poppy Reserve, *185*
Antelope Valley Indian Museum, *186*
antique shops, *38*
Anza, Juan Bautista de, *140–142*
Anza-Borrego State Park, *142-146*
archeological sites: Anza-Borrego State Park, *142-143*; Calico Early Man Site, *58, 60*; Mitchell Caverns, *64-65*; petroglyphs, *3, 25, 31*; Rainbow Basin, *55-56, 60*
avalanches, *21*

Bagley, Worth, *133-134*
bajada, defined, *18*
Baker, CA, *58-59, 61*
Ballarat, CA, *110-115, 117, 125*
Barren Ridge, *3*
Barstow, CA, *14, 56-58*
Beatty, NV, *101-102, 103-104, 117*
Beaudry, Victor, *41*
Belshaw, M.W., *41*
Big Bell (mine), *129-130*
birds, *150-151, 187*
BLM, *see* Bureau of Land Management (BLM)
Blythe intaglios, *161, 166, 167*
Bodey, Waterman "Bill," *43-44, 48*

Bodie, CA, *43-47, 48*
Boehringer, Clint, *108-110*
bookstores, *99*
borax mining, *15, 21-22*
Borax Museum, *99*
Boron, CA, *15*; cross-country route to Randsburg, *34-38*
bottle house, *108, 109*
Bullfrog, CA, *106, 110*
Burcham, Charlie, *31-32*
Bureau of Land Management (BLM), *10-11, 14, 67, 69*; camping rules, *179-180*; Desert Area Field Offices, *171-172*; off-highway vehicle areas, *172*; Regional Wild Horse & Burro Corrals, *39, 47*
Burro Schmidt's Tunnel, *24*
burros and wild horses, *39-50, 47*
Burts, Matt, *82*

Cable Road, *80, 84*
Calico Early Man Site, *58, 60*
Calico Ghost Town, *58, 60*
California Desert Protection Act (1994), *14*
California State Parks, Mojave Desert, *183-188*
camels, *75*
camping: Afton Canyon, *60*; Death Valley, *100*; Joshua Tree National Park, *137*; Mojave National Preserve, *87*; NPS and BLM rules, *179-182*; Red Rock Canyon State Park, *23*; Saddleback Butte State Park, *187*
Casebier, Dennis, *66-69, 77*
cats, endangered, *50, 52*
caverns, *64-65, 187-188*

Cedar Canyon, *76, 82*
center of the world, *159-160*
Cerro Gordo, *40-41, 43, 48*
Chemehuevis Indians, *75-76, 77-78*
China Lake, *39*
cholla cactus, *157*
Cima, CA, *63*
Cima Dome, *64*
Cima Road, *63, 64*
clothing and gear, *175-176*
Coe the Good Dragon at the Center of the World (Istel), *159-160*
Colorado Desert, *139-167*; Anza-Borrego State Park, *142-146*; description, *139-140*; legend of Pegleg Smith, *144-146*; maps, *155, 163*; Picacho Peak area, *156-160*; plants, *139*; Salton Sea, *147-154*; wildlife, *150-151*
Colorado River, *76, 147, 149, 151, 154, 158*
creosote bush, *2, 157*
Cross, Ernest, *104-107, 110*
Cudahy Camp, *20, 24*
Curry, "Gangrene Gene," *113-114, 115*

Dally, *53-54, 165*
Darwin, CA, *43, 48*
Dayton, Jim, *116*
Death Valley and the Amargosa (Lingenfelter), *89, 129*
Death Valley National Park: maps, *88-137, 103*; camping, *100, 181-182*; Death Valley Scotty, *126-131, 132*; description, *89-92*; food and supplies, *99*; hotels/motels, *99*; information, *171*; legends, *92-94*; map, *88*; Pannamint Mountains, *118-126*; plants and animals, *92*; The Racetrack, *90-91, 94-98*; safety precautions, *101-102*; temperature records, *90, 148*
Death Valley Scotty, *126-131, 132*

desert acacia, *139, 157*
desert allure, *6-7*
Desert Magazine, 146
Desert Queen Ranch, *132-133, 134, 136*
desert tortoise, *15-16*
desert towns, typical, *57*
desert travel, *173-182*; camping, *179-182*; driving tips, *174-175*; emergency supplies, *176-177*; gear and clothing, *175-176*; killer bees, *176*; land use areas, *173-174*; snakes, *176*; survival tips, *177-178*
Dumont Dunes, *59*
Dutch Boy Cleanser open pit, *21-22*

Earp, Wyatt, *162, 164, 166*
Eckles, Gerald and Janel, *161-162, 164*
eco-awareness, *10-11*, see also land use issues
Edwards, Howard Arden, *186*
Edwards Air Force Base, *36, 49, 52*
El Paso Mountains, *18*
elephant tree, *139*
emergency supplies, *176-177*
Emigrant campground, *101*
environmental concerns, *see* land use issues
exfoliation, *21*
Exotic Feline Breeding Compound, *50, 52*

fan palm, *139*
Federal Land Management and Park Offices, *170*
Felicity, CA, *159-160*
flight test centers, *49*
Floras, Pablo, *40*
Fort Mojave, *75-76*
Fort Piute, *68, 78*
fossils, *see* archeological sites
Foster, Lynn, *142*
Fremont, John, *135*

Friends of the Mojave Road, *68, 76-77*
Furnace Creek, CA, *98, 99*; campground, *100*

Garces, Francisco, *74*
Gardner, Earl Stanley, *134*
Gavilan Wash, *158*
Gaylord, E. Burdon, *129-130*
gear and clothing, *175-176*
Gem Hill, *3*
Geology Tour Road, *136*
Gerard, Julius, *128-129*
ghost towns: Bodie, *43-47, 48*; Calico Ghost Town, *58, 60*; Panamint City, *121-123, 125*
Gibbons gang, *119-121*
Goffs, CA, *66*
Goffs-Lanfair-Ivanpah Road, *63*
gold and silver mining, *26*; Bullfrog strike, *105-107*; Cerro Gordo, *40-41, 43, 48*; Gold Rock Mining District, *155-156*; Last Chance Canyon, *20*; lode gold, *28*; Panamint Mountains, *115-116, 119-121*; placer gold, *28*; Rand (Yellow Aster Mine), *26, 31-32*
Gold Rock Mining District, *155-156*
Golden Valley, *25-31*; map, *27*
Government Holes, *81-82*
Grey, Zane, *156-157*
Guide to Bodie and Eastern Sierra Historic Sites (Williams), *45-47*
gunfight at Government Holes, *81-82*

Harris, Shorty, *104-107, 109-116, 118*
Harrisburg, CA, *116, 117, 125-126*
Hart's Place, CA, *24*
Heber, Anthony, *149*
Hedges (Tumco), CA, *155, 160*
horseback riding, *187*
Horvitz, Steve, *149-151*

hot springs, *61, 70-71*
hotels/motels: Death Valley, *99, 104*; Mojave Desert, *50, 72, 87, 124*
Hoyt, Minerva, *136*
Hughs, David, *79-80*
Hyduke Mine Road, *157*

Indian Pass Road, *157*
information sources, *169-170*
intaglios, *161, 166, 167*
Istel, Jacques-André, *159-160*

jack rabbit, *2*
Jacobs, Richard, *119-121*
Johnson, Albert, *126, 128-129, 130*
Johnston, Thomas, *84*
Jones, John P., *120-121*
Joshua tree, *2, 15, 36, 135-136, 185*
Joshua Tree National Park, *131-137, 171*; camping, *137, 181-182*
Juan Bautista de Anza National Historic Trail, *141-142*

kangaroo rat, *37-38*
Keane, Jack, *105*
Kelbaker Road, *63*
Kelso, CA, *64*
Kelso Dunes, *64, 71*
Kennedy, William, *119-121*
Keys, Bill, *132-135*
killer bees, *176*
Kumeyaay tribe, *142-143*

Lancaster, CA, *49-52*
land use issues, *10-11, 14, 62-63, 173-174*; mining, *21-22, 51*
Lanfair Valley, *80-81*
Last Chance Canyon, *18-25*; map, *19*
Lawton, Frances May, *133, 134*
Lingenfelter, Richard, *89, 129*
Lippincott Mine Road, *95, 96*
Living Desert Reserve, *154*
Lockwood, Charles R., *148-149*

lode gold, *28*
Lost Gunsight Mine, *93*

Mahogany Flat campground, *101*
maps: Barstow and the Central Mojave, *55*; Beatty to Ballarat, *103*; the Blythe Intaglios, *163*; Boron to Randsburg, *35*; Death Valley, *88*; Deserts of California, *9*; Golden Valley, *27*; Last Chance Canyon, *19*; North of Yuma, *155*; Ridgecrest to Points North, *42*
Marl Springs, *83-86*
Matango Museum, *39*
McDonald, John, *122-123*
Mesquite Spring campground, *101*
mice, *37-38*
mining: borax, *15, 21-22*; environmental effects, *21-22, 51*; fraud, *128-130*; legend of Pegleg Smith, *145-146, see also* ghost towns; gold and silver mining; Rainbow Chasers
Mitchell Caverns, *64, 187-188*
Mojave Desert, *8, 13-87*; animals, *15-16, 37-38, 39-40*; Barstow and the Central Mojave, *53-61*; Boron to Randsburg, *31-38*; description, *13-18*; doing nothing, *17-18*; Golden Valley, *25-31*; hotels/motels, *72*; information center, *183-184*; Land of Dreams, *48-52*; Last Chance Canyon, *18-25*; maps, *9, 19, 29, 35, 42, 55*; Mojave National Preserve, *61-72*; Mojave Road, *72-87*; plants, *2, 15, 21*; Ridgecrest and points north, *39-48*; state parks, *183-188*
Mojave Desert Heritage and Cultural Association, *69*
Mojave Indians, *75, 77-78*
Mojave National Preserve, *61-72*; information centers, *170*
Mojave River, *58*

Mojave Road, *65, 67-69, 72-87*
Mojave Road Guide (Casebier), *68, 76, 82*
Mooers, F. M., *31-32*
Morning Star Mine Road, *63*

Nadeau, Remi, *43, 123*
National Park Service rules, *101, 181-182*
Native Americans: Antelope Valley Indian Museum, *186*; Chemehuevis Indians, *75-76, 77-78*; intaglios, *161, 166, 167*; Kumeyaay tribe, *142-143*; Mojave Indians, *75, 77-78*; Piute Indians, *77-78*; Timbesha Shoshone, *90*

ocotillo, *157*
off-highway vehicle areas, *172, 173-174*
Old Spanish Trail, *59, 92*
Olga (at Randsburg), *32-33*
Oliver, Grace, *186*
Oliver, Harry, *145-146*
outlaw gangs, *119-121, 122-123*

Palm Desert, CA, *153*
Palm Springs, CA, *153*
Palm Springs Desert Museum, *153*
Palmdale, CA, *49-52*
palo verde, *139*
Panamint City (ghost town), *121-123, 125*
Panamint Mountains, *8, 115-116, 118-126*
Pepper, Choral, *146*
petroglyphs, *3, 25*
Picacho Peak region, *156-160*
Picacho Peak State Recreation Area, *158*
Piute Creek, *79*
Piute Indians, *77-78*
Piute Mountains, *77, 80*
placer gold, *28*

plants: cactus, *157*; Colorado Desert (plants of), *139*; creosote bush, *2, 157*; desert acacia, *139, 157*; elephant tree, *139*; fan palm, *139*; Joshua tree, *2, 15, 36, 135-136, 185*; ocotillo, *157*; palo verde, *139*; poppy, *185*; salt cedar, *21*; smoke tree, *139, 157*
playas, defined, *15*
poppy, *185*
population, *16-17*
Pronuba moth, *135*
Providence Mountains, *187-188*

Quartz Hill, CA, *49*

The Racetrack, *90-91, 94-98*
racing: Willow Springs International Raceway, *52*
railroad loop, *1-2*
Rainbow Basin, *53-56, 60*
Rainbow Chasers (prospectors), *20, 26-31*
Randsburg, CA (and area), *15, 31-34*; cross-country route from Boron, *34-38*
Red Rock Canyon State Park, *18, 184*; camping, *23*
Rhyolite, NV, *104-107, 106-107, 108, 117*
Ridgecrest, CA (and area), *39-48, 124*; map, *42*
Ripley Desert Woodland, *185*
Roaring Ridge, *21, 22, 24*
Robinson, J.W. "Bill," *81-82*
rock shops, *34-35*
Rock Spring, *81*
rockhounding, *20, 34-35*

Saddleback Butte State Park, *187*
Saline Valley Road, *95-96*
salt cedar, *21*
Salt Hills, *59*

Salton Sea, *140, 147-154*; algae blooms and oxygen levels, *151-152*; origins, *148-149*; salt concentration, *149-151*; wildlife, *150-151*
Scott, Walter "Death Valley Scotty," *126-131, 132*
Scotty's Castle, *126-127, 130, 131*
Searchlight, NV, *77*
"Seldom Seen" Slim, *114-115*
Shanteler, Louie, *113-114*
Silurian Lake, *59*
silver, *see* gold and silver mining
Silver Senators, *120-121, 122-123*
singing sands (Kelso Dunes), *71*
Singleton, John, *31-32*
Skidoo, *125-126*
Small, John, *122-123*
Smith, Grant, *44-45, 46-47*
Smith, Thomas "Pegleg," *144-146*
smoke tree, *139, 157*
snakes, *176*
Soda Lake, *77, 85*
Soda Springs, *70-71, 85*
Soledad Mountain, *51*
Springer, Curtis Howe, *70-71*
Stewart, Robert, *119-121*
Stewart, William, *120-121, 122-123*
storms, desert, *26*
Stovepipe Wells, *99*; campground, *100*
Sunset campground, *100*
Surprise Canyon, *121*
survival tips, *177-178*

talc transfer station, *60 (photo)*
Teakettle Junction, *5 (photo)*
Tecopa, *59-60*
Tecopa Hot Springs, *61*
Tehachapi Loop, *1-2*
temperature records, *90, 148*
Teutonia Peak, *64*
Texas Spring campground, *100*
Thompson, Jackson, *84*

Thorndike campground, *101*
thunderstorms, *26*
Timbesha Shoshone, *90*
tortoise, desert, *15-16*
Trails End, Wyatt Earp's, *162,*
  166-167
tramway, *153-154*
travel tips, *see* desert travel
Travis, Lola, *43*
trees, *see* plants
Trona Pinnacles, *40 (photo), 48, 125*
Tropico road, *3*
Tumco (Hedges), *155, 160*
20 Mule Team Road, *36*

Ubehebe Crater, *91*

volcanic activity, *63, 91*

wagon trains: Death Valley, *92-93;*
  Mohave Road, *72-74, 78*
water, *73, 85, 153;* Salton Sink,
  147-148
websites, *169*
Whipple, Amiel Weeks, *83*

Wicht, Chris, *112, 113-114*
wild horses and burros, *39-40, 47*
wilderness designation, *see* land use
  issues
wildflowers: Antelope Valley California Poppy Reserve, *185; see also*
  plants
wildlife: birds, *150-151, 187;* desert
  tortoise, *15-16;* jack rabbit, *2;* kangaroo rat, *37-38;* killer bees, *176;*
  mice, *37-38;* Pronuba moth, *135;*
  Saddleback Butte State Park, *187;*
  Salton Sea, *150-151;* snakes, *176;*
  wild horses and burros, *39-40, 47*
Wildrose Canyon, *101, 122, 125*
Williams, George, III, *45-47*
Willow Springs International Raceway, *52*

Yellow Aster Mine, *26, 31-32*
Yucca brevifolia (Joshua tree), *2, 15,*
  36, 135-136, 185
Yuma, AZ, *154*

Zzyzx, *70-71, 85*

Adventure Guides

This signature Hunter series targets travelers eager to really explore the destination, not just visit it. Extensively researched and offering the very latest information available, *Adventure Guides* are written by knowledgeable, experienced authors, often local residents.

Adventure Guides offer the best mix of conventional travel guide and high adventure book. They cover all the basics every traveler needs – where to stay and eat, sightseeing, transportation, climate, culural issues, geography, when to go and other practicalities – followed by the adventures. Whether your idea of "adventure" is parasailing, hiking, swimming, horseback riding, hang-gliding, skiing, beachcombing or rock climbing, these books have all the information you need. The best local outfitters are listed, along with contact information. Valuable tips from the authors will save you money, headaches and hassle.

Town and regional maps make navigation easy. Photos complement the lively text. All *Adventure Guides* are fully indexed.

Adventure Guide to the Alaska Highway

Adventure Guide to Arizona

Adventure Guide to The Bahamas

Explore Belize

Adventure Guide to Bermuda

Adventure Guide to Canada's
Atlantic Provinces

Adventure Guide to the Catskills
& Adirondacks

Adventure Guide to the Cayman Islands

Adventure Guide to the Chesapeake Bay

Adventure Guide to Costa Rica

Explore the Dominican Republic

Adventure Guide to the Florida Keys
& Everglades National Park

Adventure Guide to Georgia

Adventure Guide to the
Georgia & Carolina Coasts

Adventure Guide to Hawaii

Adventure Guide to the High Southwest

Adventure Guide to Idaho

Adventure Guide to the Inside Passage
& Coastal Alaska

Adventure Guide to Jamaica

Adventure Guide to the Leeward Islands

Adventure Guide to Maine

Adventure Guide to Massuchusetts
& Western Connecticut

Adventure Guide to Michigan

Adventure Guide to Montana

Adventure Guide to Nevada

Adventure Guide to New Hampshire

Adventure Guide to Northern California

Adventure Guide to Northern Florida
& the Panhandle

Adventure Guide to Oklahoma

Adventure Guide to Orlando & Central Florida

Adventure Guide to the Pacific Northwest

Adevnture Guide to Puerto Rico

Adventure Guide to the Sierra Nevada

Adventure Guide to Southeast Florida

Adventure Guide to Tampa Bay
& Florida's West Coast

Adventure Guide to Texas

Adventure Guide to Trinidad & Tobago

Adventure Guide to Vermont

Adventure Guide to Virginia

Adventure Guide to the Yucatán